THE COOKING OF
PARMA

THE COOKING OF
PARMA

RICHARD CAMILLO SIDOLI

PHOTOGRAPHY BY SUSAN BROWN

First published in the United States of America in 1996 by
Rizzoli International Publications, Inc.
300 Park Avenue South
New York, NY 10010

Library of Congress Cataloging-in-Publication
Sidoli, Richard
The cooking of Parma / by Richard Sidoli.
p. cm.
Includes index.
ISBN 0-8478-1926-4 (hc)
1. Cookery, Italian. 2. Cookery—Italy—Parma (Province).
I. Title.
TX723.S47 1996
641.5945'44—dc20
96-18468
CIP

DESIGNED BY JOEL AVIROM
DESIGN ASSISTANT: JASON SNYDER

Printed in Italy

ACKNOWLEDGMENTS

*I*t is impossible for me to thank all the wonderful people who contributed to this book. So let me mention a few of you who share my passion for the cooking of Parma and encouraged and helped me to put it on paper.

My parents showed me the way. They gave me the tools—the traditions of our forefathers' kitchens—and their enthusiastic support. Aunt Irma Regazzi provided the little things that made the difference and instilled confidence in me like no one else could. Uncle Albert Emanuelli and Aunt Ida Sidoli Emanuelli clarified my work and validated my efforts. My in-laws, Robert and Annette Capellupo, are always there when I need them—Bob I could never do or say enough. Ralph DeLucia enabled me to appreciate what today's camera can do.

My American use of the Italian language was transferred into standard Italian by Teresa Regazzi. Conversations with Sandra Ferrari of Farfanaro in the Province of Parma assured me that my interpretations of Parma's food captured its authenticity. When a hand was needed for a photography shoot, Renzo Bonino raised his. Christopher Sidoli's historical digging added depth to my own research. The last Scapinian, Giovanni Conti, provided tales of our family's history, from the Apennines to wherever we have migrated. Robert Regazzi stressed the importance of re-creating the dishes our Grandparents Clotilde and Augustino Conti put on the table, and the Honorable Albert E. Emanuelli pushed me out of hibernation to reveal their formulas. And yes, Bruce Bozzi, it is about time.

Endless stories of Parma and numerous vacations there led me to read about the province. I found three books to be most interesting: *Storia di Compiano in Valtaro* by Gino Alpi and Ettore Rulli; *Valtaro e Valceno nell'Altomedioevo* by V. Fumagalli, G. Petracco Sicardi, and D. Ponzini; and *Parma in Tavola* by John B. Dancer.

Thanks to our friends Remo Tozzi and Gulio Sottovia, proprietors of Alps Provision in Queens, who provided the Parmigiano-Reggiano and other products that helped make this book possible. The *prosciutto di Parma* pictured on the title page came from our friends John and Maria Avitabile in Yonkers, New York.

Elizabeth (Betty), Joseph, Richard and Diane: how long are you going to put up with me?

Grazie—tante—tante—tante!

CONTENTS

Meat, Game, Poultry and Fish

FOREWORD

The cuisine of Parma, Italy, is set apart and acclaimed by travelers and gourmands. It takes a person nurtured in our community to blend the flavors precisely and to explain how you can re-create Parma's authentic taste in your kitchen. To me, the person with the knowledge, experience, and ability to share that knowledge is Richard Camillo Sidoli.

Our culinary roots, Richard's and mine, were established when our grandparents came to New York from Parma. My grandfather, Pio Bozzi, opened The Palm restaurant with John Ganzi. Richard's grandparents arrived at about the same time. His grandfather Conti opened a fine pastry shop in the Bronx, New York. Richard's other grandfather, Sidoli, opened a gourmet Italian food store across the street from the Palm and established a resort in Pine Plains, New York. My father, Bruno, went to work for his father; and Richard's father, Camillo, also joined his father. Camillo eventually became the proprietor of his own restaurant, Camillo.

Working in the same industry, our fathers understood each other's abilities and respected each other's accomplishments. Yet, when they gathered together as friends, not a word of business was spoken. Introduced through their heritage, their mutual admiration resulted in a lasting friendship. We all enjoyed the food, the music, the culture of our ancestors, and being friends.

When it was time for Richard and me to start to make our way, I went to work at the Palm, and he went to Camillo Restaurant. There he acquired the skills and knowledge to produce the taste of Parma, the sense of balanced flavors that distinguishes the dishes of our province.

Richard Camillo Sidoli enjoys unique qualities, inherent and acquired. In this book, he shares his knowledge and information and provides practical ways for everyone to put the fine dishes of Parma on the table.

BRUCE BOZZI
PARTNER, PROPRIETOR
PALM RESTAURANTS

INTRODUCTION

*I*wrote this book for all my friends who are forever asking me questions about food, particularly how the dishes from Parma, Italy, are prepared and served. Parma is the Italian province that provides us with such extraordinary products as Parmigiano-Reggiano and prosciutto di Parma, and other specialties. My friends come to me because I carry in my head a small encyclopedia of recipes from the land of my forebears—the cosmopolitan city of Parma and the surrounding rugged hills of Val Taro in the Apennine mountain range.

Why am I sought out with such questions? I was blessed, born with a wooden spoon you might say.

My story really begins with my great-grandmother, Angelina Ferrari, or Nonna Vecchia as she preferred to be called, who made the decision to leave the province of Parma and come to America. She was a farmer's daughter with no formal education but she wanted a better life for her daughters. So, in the 1890s, she left her children with her husband in their mountain hamlet and made the voyage across the Atlantic. She passed through Ellis Island, penniless but determined. She took the most logical plan of action for a woman in her predicament and sought shelter in a residence for women. At that time there was no lodging for northern Italian women speaking her dialect, and, homeless, she took refuge in the American Express stables across from New York City's Grand Central Station. Her only possessions were courage, wisdom, and a treasury of knowledge of the food of Parma. Eventually she found living quarters and a job rolling cigars. After work, she would prepare traditional meals for the single people from Parma who began to make up a circle of acquaintances old and new. Once established in New York, she sent for her family.

My great-aunt, Maria Sidoli, or Zia Maria as I called her, was quite different from Nonna Vecchia, though just as headstrong. She was the daughter of a substantial landowner and something of an adventuress who wanted more out of life than looking after her father's barnyard, garden, and house. So, off to America she went. She arrived at her brother's home in New York City in the early 1900s, enthusiastic and career-minded. I have always felt that Nonna Vecchia and Zia Maria—one a farmer, the other something of a patrician—were ideal representatives of their people and their kitchens, and their cooking was typical of their former mountain region of Parma's Val Taro.

Thanks to my ancestors, I have food in my bones, my heart, and my soul. My two grandfathers, Nonno Giuseppe Sidoli and Nonno Augustino Conti, brought their skills from Parma to New York. Nonno Giuseppe had been trained in the culinary arts, and worked in America as a chef in several first-class hotels and restaurants. He was well recognized and had a following. (One person who appreciated his talents was the great opera star Enrico Caruso.) In due time, Giuseppe opened a gourmet Italian food store and eventually became the owner of a resort in Pine Plains, New York. Nonno Augustino established a well-known Italian-French pastry shop in the Bronx. And my father, Camillo Sidoli, owned and operated an elegant restaurant, Camillo's, in midtown Manhattan for many years. Before the flavors of Italy's northern regions were fashionable in the United States, my father and two grandfathers successfully re-created the fine cuisine of Parma and the Val Taro in New York.

As for me, I was raised in the kitchen. My rattles were wooden spoons and ladles. Mixing bowls, pots, and pans were my toys. Fun and games were stirring polenta, kneading pasta dough, snapping beans, and, on special occasions, decorating cookies. My after-school treat was helping Zia Maria cook supper.

As I grew up, I always watched my grandfathers at work. Nonno Augustino talked to me about the intricate pastries he was making, often letting me take part in the process or invent some of my own. When he realized I would make my career in food, he gave me a huge book on fancy classical pastry and cake decorating. I remember with equal fondness my times with Nonno Giuseppe at his resort. After his busy summer season ended, he and his friends would gather there, and during the autumn hunting season he catered to small groups of sportsmen. This gave us the opportunity to be together. As he prepared the evening meals, he would put me on the kitchen table where I could watch and listen to him explain his cooking techniques.

I think this was how I gained my passion for preparing food. Both my grandfathers worked with love and passion, whether preparing a simple pot of soup or creating a breathtakingly decorated special cake. Their passion became mine.

As a high school student, I spent my summers working for my father at Camillo's. No job was too large or small. At college I studied culinary arts and food science and management, and, ever since, I have devoted my life to food. My skills have enabled me to satisfy the appetites of thousands of people from all walks of life with classical dishes from many lands, but my greatest successes have always involved the cooking secrets of my ancestral Parma.

Parma is a beautiful place. The city has a radiant presence with a wealth of established fine arts, performing arts, and kitchen arts. The richly cultivated countryside is punctuated by steep mountains, rolling hills, and deep forests; the area is truly a garden of plenty. Parma's people have an elegant humbleness and customs that are their own, not influenced by other provinces. The region's cookery is thus unique, incorporating a multitude of foods, all the land has to offer.

Life and tradition are long in Parma. The people are naturally health-conscious, and their diets are as beneficial today as they were in centuries past. Parma's food chemistry studies—combined with the instincts and common sense of the cooks from the country and the city, unblemished by fashionable chefs—yield delicious, healthful meals. The cooking is light, rustic, refined, and subtle. Flavors come in layers—no one taste is allowed to dominate. Our table fare enables us to experience a bounty of flavors with delicate purity.

This book is more than a collection of recipes from Nonna Vecchia and Zia Maria. Included are the wisdom and teachings of professional culinary artists from Parma. Nonno Giuseppe, Nonno Augustino, and my father combined 176 years of dedication and experience. Their instructions to me were simple—first, wash your hands, then a handful of this and a pinch of that, stir this way not that. With my watchful eyes, I learned their recipes, their secrets, and their methods. I memorized ingredients and their proportions, converting vague descriptions into easy-to-follow instructions. The result is a guidebook to better living—a collection of kitchen knowledge and recipes—unaltered over the generations. The recipes are not complicated, and their execution is usually quite simple. The aromas and flavors, however, are complex and unforgettable.

Many of us are generations removed from Parma, and too many have forgotten or failed to master its cuisine. We neglected its cookery in the era of heavy dishes and thick, rich sauces. But this is a new age. Our diets have become increasingly important to us. So, too, has our respect for heritage. This renewal of interest encourages me to pass on, to everyone who enjoys great food, the food as it originally was cooked in this remarkable province of Italy.

—R.C.S.

HISTORY AND FOLKLORE

Hannibal and his fellow Carthaginians passed through the Apennines between 218 and 217 B.C. They reached the plains of the province before the city of Parma existed. He dismounted his elephant to replenish his energy. With a *primo piatto*—first course—of cured meats from the region, his strength was revitalized. After sampling the cured leg of boar, Hannibal proclaimed that his ventursome journey from Carthage was worth its misfortunes and discomforts.

The cured boar Hannibal feasted on was the same product the Etruscans had been exporting to Greece and other parts of the civilized world for 500 years. Hannibal had discovered a tranquil setting with well-mannered, hard-working artisans who developed their art and cultivated the land. The Etruscans made and exported spears, arrows, and shields as well as grain and prosciutto. Hannibal called this place Parma, the name of the small protective shield used by his army. His appreciation of prosciutto prompted him to build a fortress to safeguard Parma's cured ham from intruders.

The Romans under Scipio finally defeated Hannibal's forces and the Italian penninsula was once again theirs. The Romans were concerned about agricultural efficiency and production. Particular attention was given to improving the cultivation of grains. Larger grains were milled to produce *laganae* (an early form of pasta), *pulmentum* (polenta), and other dishes that have their roots in Parma. The Romans said that nothing is better than bread and prosciutto. Small grains were mixed with vegetables and meat juices to make a *zuppa* or *puls*, the father of Parma's minestra.

There are scholars who say the Romans' devotion to grain brought rice to the Po Valley with some assistance from the Venetians. The introduction of rice delighted the enthusiastic Parmigiani, who immediately incorporated rice into their diet, and instantly found use for the messenger pigeon that flew in the wrong direction: It was served up in *la bomba di riso*, of which more later in this book.

The Romans also made cheese from the milk of goats and sheep, the latter most likely what we know as Pecorino Romano. According to some scholars it was during Roman times that the Parmigiani began to produce cheese from cows' milk alone. According to other learned people it was the Parmigiani who introduced the cows' milk cheese to the Romans. Here, Julius Caesar was thrilled with the new taste of wild asparagus and butter.

Most of the province of Parma lies in the Apennines; the Romans considered the mountains theirs and ventured in. There, they met people clad in animal skins whom they described as robust and tall shepherds, hunters, and fishermen. The natives lived off the bounty of the land: game, fish, fresh fruits, wild vegetables, and light dairy products. These early Parmigiani were a tenacious, sentimental group, open, strong, loyal warriors who never gave in to the empire. The Romans reached the Valle Padana, but not the Taro. They left the mountains saying the people could manage without them and never even tasted the *porcini* mushrooms of the Val Taro.

During the Roman Empire the word of the region's bounty spread, and as the empire declined, people flocked there. First came the Goths, who pushed out the Romans. From the east came the Byzantines, throwing spears and wielding swords for a slice of prosciutto and *laganae*. Shortly after, the Longobards swarmed into the region. They were big meat eaters, and between wild game and farm animals, there was plenty to feast on. And the Longobards gave creative cooks the incentives that brought a greater variety to the meats, which they grilled, roasted, potted, stuffed, and boiled. They were particularly fond of various meats and vegetables boiled together, a dish known as *bollito misto*, which remains a signature of Parma's cuisine. So they stayed.

In time, the Parmigiani gave a great deal of thought to diversifying their diet and to the cooking of food. Culinary techniques utilizing vinegar, wine, and herbs were improved for medicinal purposes as well as for the preservation of foods. *Stracotto*, a form of stewed or potted meats, is one of the most important developments. There is also evidence that around this time pasta was refined. During the Longobard era pasta may have been flattened and special filled pastas were developed for the nobility. Pasta filled with meat and meat essences—now known as *anolini*—was eaten in the winter, and pasta filled with greens—*tortelli di erbette* or *tortie*—was enjoyed in the summer.

The Apennine people continued to live as woodsmen, hunters, shepherds, and fishermen. They also gathered fruits and vegetables, both cultivated and uncultivated. For the most part, the thick forests and steep hillsides kept the mountain inhabitants, particularly of the Val Taro–Val Ceno area, apart from the rest of Parma. However, a few people traveled in and out. Germanics wandered in and some became part of the community. Travelers passing through sought shelter, and were treated to *puls*, along with all manner of grains, game, pork, poultry, fish, fresh produce, *porcini* mushrooms, herbs, and probably pastas such as *tortie*.

Most of us were taught that the dark ages, which extended from about A.D. 400 to about 1000, was a period of intellectual stagnation. But in 962, one Bishop Umberto received a diploma or certificate from Otto the Great, Holy Roman Emperor, which decreed him to begin "universal" studies for the improvement of the Parmesan community. This may have been the first step toward the formation of the university. An assortment of fields was chosen; one was *magiche alchimie culinarie*—"the magical alchemy of cookery."

As monasteries became the centers of the community, monks became absorbed in food science. They were concerned about the growing population and worked to improve agriculture and the care and breeding of animals; their achievements were shared with the community. The aim of their research was to maintain the highest quality of food. They developed methods to guide, stimulate, and influence techniques. Scientists studying fruits, nuts, and sugar improved and developed an assortment of sweets and liquors. Pharmaceutical studies and Arabic translations provided the significant information needed to make frozen sweets.

Advancements in agriculture and food created prosperity, and the arts and culture were maturing. It was time to build in the city of Parma. In the tenth century, a beautiful cathedral, St. John's, was constructed. By the eleventh century the population outgrew the cathedral, and the magnificent Duomo was begun. A towering baptistry was built across the piazza. A merchants' hall was established to accommodate the flourishing market. And, for the statesmen, a city hall and a bustling town square sprang up.

In this era some families prospered and gained political authority. In time, they were in a position of real political strength, and evolved into a nobility that obtained power from the Holy Roman Empire. Patrician families in the mountains and forests governed independently of the city. The families in the city and surrounding environs were not militaristic and they yielded territory to the barrage of storming troops from outside factions: Milan, Spain, France, and Austria. Parma was not a priority for the incoming leaders, and they assigned their subordinates to govern the region. Their main interests were to promote the arts and whatever would increase their wealth, and to party with the courtesans. The noble banquets were festive affairs, complete with jesters, musicians, and an endless array of food. By this time Parma had a wealth of resources for gala functions. A new assortment of pasta included an additional filled variety and the quantity and quality of sweets were outrageous; *gelato* and *sorbetto* were created for the gentry. Techniques were simplified by homemakers, who created *zabaione*, sweet tarts, and preserved fruits.

Steep mountains, thick forests, and a free spirit kept the people in the Apennines relatively independent of the city. The Landi family acquired much land and wealth in Val Taro–Val Ceno. From the mid-1200s to 1762, they provided good administration, fair justice, free schools, stamped money, and medicine; the area was an autonomous community. At the marketplace, people traded goods, foodstuffs, and ideas from within and outside the region. From the hamlet Sidolo, high in the mountains, descended the Sidoli family. They moved in and out of the mountains, and set up a haven for travelers in the neighboring hamlet of Scapini on the Tontira River. Here, a weary visitor—whether a donkey-train driver, or a duchess—could eat, drink, sleep, and be merry. Some found this tranquil small garden, secluded from the rest of Italy, an escape. Everyone feasted on the products provided by the uncultivated and cultivated pastures, mountains, valleys, and streams, which were simply prepared over wood fires. There were seasonal delights: In late spring wild strawberries sprouted through the soil; later in the year bouquets of mushrooms scented the air; chestnuts were roasted, sweetened, milled into flour, and wrapped in pasta; superb pears were cooked in sweetened wine.

Although they had no way of knowing, the Parmigiani had perfectly laid the groundwork for the onslaught of unknown and exciting foods about to come from the New World. The most important arrivals were the vegetables; native vegetables were constantly being refined so that established traditions and flavoring techniques were easily adapted to the new ones—peppers, potatoes, squashes, tomatoes. New spices, however, were disregarded in favor of the already-entrenched local and exotic spices and herbs that blended well with the new foods. Products from the wild terrain of the Apennines also meshed well, particularly the mushrooms. Parmesan cheese blended perfectly with the fashionable new vegetables. The chestnut, an essential part of the diet, was used to make *gnocchi* before potatoes were. Potato *gnocchi* with mushrooms, *zucchini alla Parmigiana*, squash-filled pasta, and eggplant baked in tomato sauce are just a few of the culinary marriages between the Old World and the New. And let us not overlook milled corn for polenta, which was originally made with oats, barley, and wheat.

In 1796 Napoleon, with his troops, rode into Parma on his white horse. As emperor, he abolished the city-state family command in Parma and cautiously introduced changes to revive lagging resources. A sweet tooth emperor, he favored *millefoglie*, the thin crispy pastry superb with pastry cream. In 1815 Napoleon surrendered to the British and was exiled to St. Helena. His wife, Maria Luisa of Austria, adored the province, and the Congress of Vienna awarded her the duchy of Parma.

Duchess Maria Luisa, beloved by the people of Parma, administered policies that benefited the welfare of the public. She provided new or improved living conditions for her subjects and avoided political or other opposition in the Apennines by gaining the trust of prominent families such as Rossi-Sidoli, Alpi, Beoloraglia, Contù. She rewarded them by constructing or enriching their palaces. On her journeys to Val Taro–Val Ceno she often rested in Scapini.

At this point, Parma's lore became entwined with my family's. At the rest area run by the Sidolis, the duchess made a special friend. Together they rode and hunted the fields and the forests; she used an English-made, ladies' .410-gauge shotgun. In Prague the duchess had a special 14-gauge Damascus-steel shotgun, with a gold-inlaid hunting scene, made as a gift for her friend.

It would be interesting to go back in time and hear from the people of the now-ghost hamlet Scapini. Maria Luisa, like others who passed through the region, satisfied her appetite with provincial fare. Among her favorite dishes were pheasant and polenta; trout sautéed with vinegar; risotto with white wine; *tortie* with a white sauce; fine veal envelopes filled with prosciutto, Parmigiano, and herbs; and *mille-foglie* and strawberries.

An outdoors woman, the duchess fished the Parma, the Taro, and the Ceno rivers. As the snows of Mount Pelpi melt, the Tontira stream that runs by Scapini rises, and there she would visit. My great-grandfather Francesco Sidoli proudly regaled his children with stories of his boyhood experiences with the elderly duchess. Her servants would set a table under her favorite walnut tree so that she could eat *al fresco*, and little Francesco would join her and listen to tales of the forest and rivers.

There were also equestrian adventures to the summit of Mount Pelpi, where the duchess once took out a knife and carved her initials into a tree. There were picnics of the local *torta*, grilled polenta, Parma's famous cured meats, and wild strawberries, and the duchess would view the magnificent panoramic vista of her domain.

Today the Glauco Lombardi Museum in the city of Parma displays Maria Luisa's fishing gear. I inherited the two guns.

THE COOKING OF
PARMA

ANTIPASTI

Parma's antipasti offer more than prosciutto di Parma, *our region's famous air-cured ham, or prosciutto and melon. Everywhere there are magnificent arrays of various other cured meats.* Prosciutto di cinghiale—*wild boar— is one example, but the recipe cannot be duplicated away from the Apennines because it is made from the local wild boar and cured in the pure mountain air. Cured meats themselves, however, are just part of any antipasto assortment. A variety of* torta—*in Parma's Apennine Mountains this usually means vegetables or rice in a special dough—is also typical. Whenever possible, I like to serve antipasti on wood or marble surfaces.*

Funghi Marinati

Marinated Mushrooms

SERVES 4 TO 6

A plate of antipasti is not complete unless marinated mushrooms are included. They are easy to prepare, though the marinating process takes a little time.

10 ounces small button mushrooms, wiped clean if necessary

1 onion, cut up

3 cloves garlic, smashed

2 tablespoons allspice

¼ teaspoon dried basil

¼ teaspoon dried thyme

4 bay leaves

½ tablespoon whole peppercorns

Juice of 1 lemon

2 tablespoons red-wine vinegar

4 tablespoons olive oil

At least 1 tablespoon salt

Chopped fresh parsley

Fill a pot with 3 cups water, onion, garlic, allspice, herbs, peppercorns, lemon juice, vinegar, oil, and salt. Bring the water to a boil and add the mushrooms. Bring the water to a vigorous boil and remove the pot from the heat. Let the mushrooms and marinade cool to room temperature and put in an airtight container. Cover the mixture and refrigerate at least overnight, or up to 4 days.

Before serving, remove the mushrooms from the marinade with a strainer or slotted spoon, arrange in a serving dish, and top with parsley.

PÂTÉ DI PARMA

𐤏𐤏𐤏𐤏𐤏𐤏𐤏𐤏𐤏

PARMA'S LIVER PÂTÉ
SERVES 10

The French have their *pâté de foie gras*. We Parmigiani have our own pâté. In past times, pâté was an aristocratic delicacy; today it is for all who enjoy good food. Parma's pâté is delightful as an antipasto or served alone as a between-meals treat—fantastic with a bottle of rosé and a special friend.

As an apprentice at Camillo Restaurant, it was my job to purée the pâté. One day, Mr. C. himself (my father) walked into the kitchen and said to me, "Our patrons are pleased with the delicate taste of this pâté. The preparation for this dish was given to me by my father. It is never to be altered in any way whatsoever."

Nonno Giuseppe brought this recipe with him to America from Parma in 1897, and to this day it has never been "altered in any way whatsoever."

> Juice of 1 lemon plus an additional ⅜ cup fresh lemon juice
> 1½ pounds chicken livers
> 3 tablespoons olive oil
> ½ medium onion, chopped
> 1 slice (1 ounce) *pancetta* (Italian bacon), chopped
> 1 whole scallion, trimmed and thinly sliced
> ½ teaspoon dried oregano
> 1 teaspoon dried basil
> 1 bay leaf
> ½ teaspoon dried tarragon
> 1 tablespoon chopped fresh parsley
> Salt and pepper
> ¾ cup Marsala or sweet Sherry
> ½ cup chicken broth (page 64) or good-quality store-bought
> 4 tablespoons melted clarified butter (see note below)

ACCOMPANIMENTS:

> Toasts or *grissini*
> Lemon wedges

Add the juice of the lemon to a bowl of cold water and rinse the livers. Drain the livers and pat dry. Heat the oil in a 2-inch-deep sauté pan until hot and carefully add the onion and *pancetta*. Cook the mixture over medium heat until the onion is translucent, stir in the scallion, herbs, livers, and salt and pepper to taste, and cook for 2 minutes. Add ½ cup Marsala and ¼ cup additional lemon juice and let sizzle for about 45 seconds. Add the broth and cook until the livers are well done, about 20 minutes. (The livers should have lost any tinge of pink and the liquid should be reduced by about 85%.)

Purée the liver mixture in a blender or food processor and transfer to the bowl of a mixer fitted with a paddle attachment. On medium speed slowly drizzle in remaining ¼ cup Marsala alternately with remaining ⅛ cup lemon juice and the butter until the mixture is blended well. The mixture will be smooth and light.

Pour the mixture into a small (2 to 2½ cups) mold or bowl and refrigerate overnight, or until firm. To remove the pâté from the mold, dip the mold in and out of hot water, cover it with a serving plate, invert it, and lift the mold off. (It may be necessary to gently loosen the sides of the pâté from the mold.) The pâté may be a centerpiece for an antipasto platter or served separately with accompaniments.

Note: To clarify butter, slowly melt it, skim off the foam from the surface, and set aside to cool. Pour off the clear (clarified) butter from the residue that settles.

ABOUT TORTA

Anyone who has ever experienced Parma's *torta* instantly becomes addicted. Prepared and served with great pride in the Apennine Mountain areas of Val Taro and Val Ceno, it is the specialty of the people there, baked in a dough that is found only in their *paese*. Spinach is the most popular variety, but everyone has another favorite. Mine is rice, or is it potato? Every year, I eagerly await the first winter squash so I can make a *torta di zucca*. In my hands, a pretty head of Savoy cabbage ends up as *torta di cavolo di Savoia*. When a traditional menu is served in the mountain villages, torta is always included; in fact two kinds are usually served. Often a simple picnic basket is enhanced with *torta*. At festive gatherings everyone brings his own *torta*; there is an unspoken competitive spirit among the women, who almost invariably make torta; the men don't seem to be quite as good at it. *Torta* is as ubiquitous for us as quiche is for the French.

Torta recipes in any form are quite difficult to obtain from anyone. Whenever I asked anyone about his or her version, I would be told "My grandmother showed me." I tried for years to get a recipe from my mother. Finally, in desperation, when my boys were nine and eleven years old, I asked them if Grandma Marie could teach them how to make *torta*. They looked at each other and with enthusiasm agreed.

Now we have Nonna Vecchia's exact instructions to her granddaughter, Marie. Most likely, Nonna Vecchia's teacher was her grandmother.

PASTA E FONDAMENTALI PER TORTA

TORTA DOUGH AND
BASIC PREPARATION

*T*he key to this excellent dough is to work it as little as possible, then let it rest, covered, while the filling is being prepared. (Machine-made dough requires a longer rest period.) The dough can even rest a few days in the refrigerator. I use an extra-long Italian rolling pin that is the thickness of a baseball bat to roll the dough quite thin. Not long ago, I walked into my cousin Ida's kitchen in Farfanaro, Italy, and found the women rolling out dough with a pasta machine. Their baking pans were whatever sizes and shapes were available, so we had all sizes and shapes of *torta*—round, square, and rectangular. I guess they are more advanced cooks than we are here in the States.

> **2 cups flour**
> **½ teaspoon salt**
> **½ cup plus I tablespoon water**
> **4 tablespoons plus ½ teaspoon olive oil**

Preheat the oven to 425° F.

Put the flour and salt in a bowl and pour in the water and 4 tablespoons of oil. Mix together until a dough is formed (do not overwork the dough). Let the dough rest at least 20 minutes, or up to overnight. On a lightly floured table or board roll out the dough thinly (about the thickness of 2 sheets of paper). Spread the remaining ½ teaspoon of oil in a 15- by 11-inch baking pan and put the dough in the pan, leaving a 3-inch overhang on all sides.

Note: *Torta* is usually baked at 425° F; however, if the oven is already in use at a lower temperature, *torta* adapts well. It will just take a little longer to bake. In any case, it is best to let *torta* stand 30 minutes or more before cutting and serve it warm. Reheated leftover *torta* maintains its quality.

TORTA DI SPINACI

SPINACH TORTA

SERVES 6 TO 8

4 pounds fresh spinach or 4 (10-ounce) packages frozen spinach, thawed

4 tablespoons butter

½ medium onion, chopped

3 whole scallions, trimmed and thinly sliced

6 ounces very fresh *mascarpone* or other soft cheese

½ cup freshly grated Parmigiano-Reggiano

¼ cup milk

Salt and pepper

2 eggs

I recipe *torta* dough (page 9)

Preheat the oven to 425° F.

If using fresh spinach wash well in cold water. In a large pot bring about 3 inches salted water to a boil and add spinach. Cook the spinach, covered, about 7 minutes, or until *al dente*, stirring once or twice. Drain the spinach immediately and refresh under cold water. Drain the spinach again and squeeze out excess water. Chop the spinach and put it in a large bowl. Melt the butter in a sauté pan, add the onion and scallions, and cook over medium heat until the onion is translucent.

Add the cheeses, onion mixture, milk, and salt and pepper to taste to the spinach. Beat the eggs and add three fourths of them to the spinach mixture, mixing well.

Note: The filling may be prepared I day before the *torta* is assembled.

Roll out the dough and prepare the pan according to the instructions on page 9. Using a pastry brush, brush the top of the *torta* with the remaining beaten egg. Bake the *torta* until the crust is golden brown.

Note: Other greens can be combined with the spinach. My mother sometimes made a version using three parts spinach to one part Swiss chard. And when I cook for Southerners, they appreciate it when collards are substituted. A small handful (about ⅓ cup) of steamed rice blended in with the spinach is also a nice touch.

STRACCHINO E MASCARPONE

When I was growing up, the use of cream cheese in Italian dishes seemed natural to me. But when I became a culinary student and kitchen apprentice, I realized my family and *paesani* were the only Italians who seemed to use cream cheese, which at the time was confusing.

One summer years ago I was touring Italy and visited my parents, who were vacationing in Farfanaro. Of course, my mother prepared torta for me. A sassy son I was and asked, "Where did you get the cream cheese?" Dad responded, "Here they have plenty of cream cheese, and it's the best."

The first chance I had, I visited a local cheese shop and, later, one in the city of Parma. Sure enough, they all carried a cheese that looked like cream cheese, but when I tasted some I immediately realized the difference: The cheese I was eating, *stracchino*, was smoother than cream cheese, and light and creamy when fresh, with a little tang.

Back in the early 1980s an associate of mine told me of a great new cheese from Italy, *mascarpone*. He said how well it worked in different dishes—appetizers, main courses, even desserts. Upon trying it, I found to my surprise and joy it was similar to that fresh cheese I had once tasted in Italy.

I now understand why my family used cream cheese in place of *stracchino* or *mascarpone*. From the 1890s to 1980s we were not aware of these cheeses in the United States: Because of their perishable nature, they were not available at the time. In the cooking of Parma, though, *stracchino* and *mascarpone* blend fantastically with other ingredients. The cheeses are used a little differently but are often interchangeable. In the following recipes, *stracchino* may be used, but *mascarpone* is more popular and desirable. If that is not possible, feel free to substitute cream cheese. Both *stracchino* and *mascarpone* must be used when very fresh.

TORTA DI RISO

1¼ cup raw rice

4 tablespoons butter

4 whole scallions, trimmed and sliced

1 medium zucchini, cleaned but not peeled

6 ounces very fresh *mascarpone* or other soft cheese

¾ cup freshly grated Parmigiano-Reggiano

¾ cup milk

Salt and pepper

3 eggs

1 recipe *torta* dough (page 9)

Preheat the oven to 425° F.

Steam or boil the rice until it is *al dente*, drain it, and set aside. Melt the butter in sauté pan, carefully add the scallions and sauté them briefly over medium heat. Dice the zucchini. When the scallions are limp, stir in the zucchini and remove the pan from the heat.

Put the rice, scallions, and zucchini in a bowl and add the cheeses, milk, and salt and pepper to taste. Beat the eggs and add three fourths of them to the rice mixture, mixing well.

Note: The filling may be prepared 1 day before the *torta* is assembled.

Roll out the dough and prepare the pan according to the instructions on page 9. Using a pastry brush, brush the top of the *torta* with the remaining beaten egg. Bake the *torta* until the crust is golden brown.

TORTA DI PATATE

POTATO TORTA

SERVES 6 TO 8

2½ pounds russet potatoes, scrubbed but not peeled

6 tablespoons butter

½ medium onion, chopped

⅔ cup washed and chopped leek

6 ounces very fresh *mascarpone* or other soft cheese

⅔ cup freshly grated Parmigiano-Reggiano

¾ cup milk

Salt and pepper

2 eggs

1 recipe *torta* dough (page 9)

Preheat the oven to 425° F. Boil, bake, or microwave the potatoes until just tender. Melt the butter in a sauté pan, carefully add the onion and leek, and cook over medium heat until soft but not browned.

Peel the potatoes and pass through a ricer into a bowl. Add the onion mixture, cheeses, milk, and salt and pepper to taste. Beat the eggs and add three fourths of them to the potato mixture.

Note: The filling may be prepared 1 day before the *torta* is assembled.

Roll out the dough, and prepare the pan according to the instructions on page 9. Using a pastry brush, brush the top of the *torta* with the remaining beaten egg. Bake the *torta* until the crust is golden brown.

Torta di Zucca

*Z*ucca is an Italian winter squash. The most popular variety used for cooking in Italy is actually an offspring of the American pumpkin. Its shell ranges in color, and the flesh is a deep orange. Mom always substituted pumpkin when it was in season, but butternut squash is also an excellent alternative.

4 pounds *zucca*, pumpkin, or butternut squash
4 tablespoons butter
2 whole scallions, trimmed and thinly sliced
1 tablespoon chopped fresh basil
1 teaspoon freshly grated nutmeg
4 ounces very fresh *mascarpone* or other soft cheese
¾ cup freshly grated Parmigiano-Reggiano
½ cup milk
3 eggs
Salt and pepper
1 recipe *torta* dough (page 9)

Preheat the oven to 425° F.

Steam, bake, or microwave the squash until just tender. Melt the butter in a sauté pan over medium heat and add the scallions. When the scallions are limp, stir in the basil and remove the pan from the heat.

Let the squash cool slightly. Cut the squash in half, remove the seeds, and scoop out the flesh. Pass the squash through a ricer into a bowl. Add the scallions, basil, nutmeg, cheeses, milk, and salt and pepper to taste to the squash mixture, mixing well. Beat the eggs and add three fourths of them to the squash mixture.

Note: The filling may be prepared 1 day before the *torta* is assembled.

Roll out the dough and prepare the pan according to the instructions on page 9. Using a pastry brush, brush the top of the *torta* with the remaining beaten egg. Bake the *torta* until the crust is golden brown.

Torta di Cavalo di Savoia

Savoy Cabbage Torta

SERVES 6 TO 8

3 pounds Savoy cabbage

4 tablespoons butter

1½ to 2 cups sliced onion

4 ounces very fresh *mascarpone* or other soft cheese

½ cup freshly grated Pamigiano-Reggiano

¼ cup milk

Salt and pepper

2 eggs

1 recipe *torta* dough (page 9)

Preheat the oven to 425° F.

Core the cabbage, cut it into 3-inch-square pieces, and wash in cold water. In a large pot bring about 3 inches salted water to a boil and add the cabbage. Cook the cabbage until just tender (do not overcook). Drain the cabbage and refresh under cold water. Drain the cabbage again and squeeze out excess water. Put the cabbage in a bowl.

Melt the butter in a sauté pan, add the onion and cook over medium heat until translucent. Add the onion, cheeses, milk, and salt and pepper to taste to the cabbage. Beat the eggs and add three fourths of them to the cabbage mixture, mixing well.

Roll out the dough and prepare the pan according to the instructions on page 9. Using a pastry brush, brush the top of the *torta* with the remaining beaten egg. Bake the *torta* until the crust is golden brown.

ANTIPASTO DI RAPE E POMODORI

WHITE TURNIP AND TOMATO ANTIPASTO

SERVES 4 TO 6

*M*y father would begin a meal with this light dish. This combination also teams well with other antipasti.

2 medium white turnips

3 beefsteak tomatoes

1 tablespoon red-wine vinegar

Juice of ½ lemon

5 tablespoons olive oil

Salt and pepper

2 tablespoons chopped fresh basil

4 tablespoons chopped fresh parsley

Green part of 1 scallion, thinly sliced

Place 1 quart water and a pinch of salt in a deep pot and bring to a boil. Peel the turnips and slice ¼-inch thick. Add the turnips to the boiling water and cook until just tender. Drain the turnips immediately. Refresh the turnips under cold water and drain again. Wash and slice the tomatoes ¼-inch thick. Put the turnips and tomatoes into the refrigerator.

Mix together the vinegar, lemon juice, oil, and salt and pepper to taste in a bowl. Mix together the basil, parsley, and scallion in another bowl.

Arrange the turnips in a serving dish and top with the tomatoes. Drizzle the vinaigrette over and sprinkle with the herb mixture.

ANTIPASTI ASSORTITI

ASSORTED APPETIZERS

SERVES 4 TO 6

*I*n the province of Parma one thinks first of *antipasti assortiti*, cured meats often combined with some fruit and cheese. *Coppa, culatello, pancetta, prosciutto di cinghiale*, and salami are among the cured meats available, and at least three are usually offered. The meats (always cut fresh and never rolled or folded, for that would damage the texture) are delicately and systematically arranged on a platter. If fruit or cheese accompany the meats they are traditionally placed in the center. Below is a selection of meats along with the fruits that complement them best. What you won't find outside Parma is *culatello, prosciutto di cinghiale*, and the local salami which is the leanest salami I have ever seen in Italy.

> I cantalope or casaba melon
> 6 fresh figs, if available
> ¼ pound *coppa*, thinly sliced
> ¼ pound salami, thinly sliced
> ¼ pound *pancetta*, thinly sliced
> ¼ pound *cotechino*, cooked and sliced
> ¼ pound *prosciutto di Parma*, thinly sliced

Cut the melon in half, remove the skin and the seeds, and slice. Arrange the melon slices next to each other at one end of a platter. Clean the figs and slice them lengthwise. Arrange the figs, flesh sides up, across the middle of the melon slices. Arrange the *coppa* on another section of the platter, followed by the salami, *pancetta, cotechino*, and the *prosciutto di Parma*, which may be a little puffed up.

OVERLEAF, CLOCKWISE
FROM TOP: *Stuffed
Artichoke, Parma's Liver
Pâté, Prosciutto and other
cured meats, Spinach Torta,
Pumpkin Torta, Grilled
Polenta*

CARCIOFI RIPIENI

*T*his antipasto stands alone, makes a statement. I have converted many people into artichoke enthusiasts with my style of stuffed artichokes.

6 large artichokes

Juice of 1 lemon

3 tablespoons butter

⅓ cup chopped fresh *porcini* mushrooms

2 whole scallions, trimmed and sliced

½ cup dry white wine

2 to 3 tablespoons dry bread crumbs

¾ cup milk

½ cup meat broth (page 65) or good-quality store-bought

5 ounces new peas (fresh or frozen)

2 tablespoons freshly grated Parmigiano-Reggiano

Salt and pepper

Cut the stems off the artichokes and set aside. Discard the outer shaggy discolored leaves from the artichokes. Trim ½- to ¾-inch from the artichoke tops. Turn the artichokes upside-down and with a sharp knife shave the tips off the leaves. Spread the middle leaves apart and with a paring knife, melon-baller, or espresso spoon scoop out the choke, the tough, hairy leaves at the center. Rinse the artichokes under cool water and turn them upside-down to drain.

Fill a deep pot with about 2 inches of water, the lemon juice, and a pinch of salt. Put the artichokes, tops up, and stems into the water. Bring the water to a boil and cook the artichokes, covered, for 40 minutes to 1 hour, or until a leaf can be plucked off easily. Drain the artichokes and set aside. The artichokes may be prepared up to this point a day or so in advance.

Preheat the oven to 375° F. Melt the butter in a saucepan. Chop the artichoke stems, add to the melted butter with the mushrooms and scallions, and sauté over medium heat until tender, but not browned. Add the wine and continue to cook until the liquid is reduced by half. Add the broth and cook until the liquid is reduced by one third. Mix in the bread crumbs, milk, and peas, and cook until the peas are tender. Add the cheese and season the mixture with salt and pepper to taste.

Separate the leaves at the center of each artichoke and stuff the cavity with the filling. Stuff the remaining filling among the outer leaves. Put the artichokes in a shallow baking pan and bake until hot, about 15 minutes. Serve the artichokes hot.

ASPARAGI CONDITI CON OLIO, LIMONE, E ACETO ROSSO

ASPARAGUS VINAIGRETTE

YIELDS ABOUT 1 CUP

*T*his vinaigrette from my Nonno Giuseppe is an extremely versatile condiment that is used to enhance many dishes, including *bollito misto* (mixed boiled meats). Here it is served over asparagus, an easy dish in which cooking the egg is the most difficult and time-consuming aspect of the preparation.

I egg
I cup roasted red peppers
I½ tablespoons capers
½ medium tomato (half green is best)
I gherkin or *cetriolino* (little cucumber)
Green part of 2 scallions, very thinly sliced (or an equal amount of chives)
½ teaspoon dry mustard
Juice of ½ lemon
2 tablespoons red-wine vinegar
⅓ cup olive oil
Salt and pepper
Asparagus, cooked and cooled (page 132)

Boil the egg 15 minutes, let it cool, and remove the shell. Pass the hard-boiled egg, roasted peppers, capers, tomato, and gherkin through a grinder or finely chop in a food processor (do not over process). Put the mixture in a bowl and add the scallions. Gently stir in the mustard, lemon juice, vinegar, oil, and salt and pepper to taste.

Arrange the asparagus on a platter and ladle some vinaigrette over the middle third of the stalks. Any remaining vinaigrette may be kept in a tightly sealed container, refrigerated.

POLENTA ALLA GRIGLIA

GRILLED POLENTA
SERVES 4

*T*his great is dish usually enjoyed as an antipasto, and is perfect as part of an al fresco meal, or tucked into a picnic basket. Grill the polenta outdoors if possible. For this preparation, I prefer coarse corn meal.

> I cup coarsely ground corn meal
> I cup chicken broth (page 64) or good-quality store-bought
> 2 tablespoons butter
> ½ cup chopped chives or green parts of scallions
> ½ cup freshly grated Parmigiano-Reggiano
> Salt and pepper
> About ⅓ cup olive oil

Prepare polenta according to the instructions on page 29, using the corn meal, broth, and 3 cups water. Just before removing the polenta from the heat, stir in the butter, chives, and cheese, and season with salt and pepper to taste.

Prepare a grill or preheat the broiler. Spread the cooked polenta on a 10- by 12-inch baking sheet. Cool the polenta to room temperature and put in the refrigerator until firm. Cut the chilled polenta into 2- by 3-inch pieces and brush lightly with oil. Grill or broil the polenta until brown and crispy on both sides.

POLENTA,
RISOTTO,
PASTA AND
GNOCCHI

POLENTA

Polenta can be traced back to the Etruscans. According to legend, the Roman legions were at their best after a meal of pulmentum, *the dish of oats, barley, wheat—whatever grains were available—that was an early incarnation of polenta. Since the introduction of corn to Italy and the rest of Europe, polenta has been made with corn-meal. In some places in Italy, cornmeal is referred to as* granoturco, *because it was once erroneously thought to be of Turkish origin.*

Northern Italy's fertile soil and climate are ideal for the cultivation of corn. From early on, farmers appreciated the economics of growing corn, and millers ground it into farina di granoturco. *Polenta quickly became a food staple; in some communities, more polenta is eaten than pasta. Because of my background, when I was a young man the men in the old barbershop in our neighborhood called me "Polentino." Years ago, the self-proclaimed aristocrats referred to polenta as food for the peasants and, indeed, wheat was far more expensive. Today, chefs look to serve specialty dishes, and polenta has become an epicurean delight in even the most exclusive restaurants. For those of us who have always eaten polenta, it is simply part of our diet, fried, baked, or grilled, and excellent with sauces. Customarily, polenta complements the entrée's sauce.*

Risotto

Risotto is an Italian way of preparing rice. Some scholars believe that it all began when rice was brought to Italy from Asia Minor, while others tell us that it was introduced to Italy by the Saracens. In any case, the Etruscans developed the cultivation of rice—and the unique texture of Italian rice—in the Po Valley. The Etruscans also developed the cooking technique for risotto. Later the bourgeoisie claimed risotto as their dish, and a poor housewife could trade a small bag of dried mushrooms for a sack of rice.

Italians do more with rice than simply boil and serve. The range of risotto is such that it may be delicately or robustly flavored, depending on its purpose in a meal or the whim of the cook. Risotto is flavored before cooking and afterward; broth is used rather than plain water. Risotto is always al dente but also creamy (never mushy), and its velvety texture blends the flavors with which it is cooked.

I often am asked "What is the best rice for risotto?" There are traditionalists who say Arborio and others who choose Carnaroli. I have friends and relatives from Piemonte, Milan, and Parma who prefer a maximum risotto asciutto, which is quite dry and obtained from the hardest long-grain rice. Whenever someone I know is coming from Italy, I ask him to bring back riso dallari or risi tipici Emiliani.

When I am in Parma, I buy my Emilian rice at Supermercato Sigma Sidoli. In other words, we each tend to develop our own preference. Arborio is the softest grain, producing the creamiest risotto. If in doubt, first use Arborio, then try the others. My own order of preference is Emiliano, Carnaroli, Arborio.

Risotto was a specialty of Zia Maria's; her various preparations were exceptional. A frugal shopper, Zia would buy the least-expensive rice at the market, generally a medium grain. Risotto served with roast chicken is not the same risotto served with roast lamb, which in turn differs from risotto cooked for osso buco. Risotto may accompany the entrée, as with osso buco (page 88), or be served as a primo piatto, in place of pasta.

PASTA

Thinking of pasta, I often recall a conversation with Zia Maria when I was just a schoolboy. When she asked what I was learning in school, I told her we were studying about Italian explorers, and that my teacher told us Marco Polo brought spaghetti to Italy from China. Zia, matter-of-factly, said, "Si. Si. Did your teacher tell you Marco Polo brought rice to China?"

In fact, pasta was well established in Italy by the time of the Roman Empire, centuries before Marco Polo traveled to China. Cicero was fond of a ribbon-type pasta, lagganum, *which, they say, resembled today's* tagliatelle. *It is also said that the Roman hierarchy, while constructing Via Emilia, feasted on* lagganum, *which may have been an early type of lasagna.*

Parma's pastamakers are renowned. Their pasta is fresh, not dried, and is always served with sauces that are usually light—generally white but sometimes brown from the essence of meat or vegetables. Only occasionally is a red sauce used. Filled pasta is the most popular in all of Parma, and the most typical fillings are chestnut flour, greens, poultry, beef, or combinations thereof, but sausage or other dominating flavors are never used. Sauces are determined by the fillings.

POLENTA BASICS

Traditionally, polenta was prepared by slowly pouring cornmeal from one hand into boiling water while stirring and stirring and stirring with the other. A silent prayer was offered up to prevent lumping, and an hour or more was scheduled for cooking; it was a ritual.

The following method, which almost entirely eliminates stirring and cuts the cooking time dramatically, became obvious to me a number of years ago. My chef was preparing polenta the old-fashioned way, and I was preparing pastry cream. It occurred to me that the procedure might decrease considerably the time, energy, and lumping potential of cooking polenta. We tried it and it worked.

What we discovered is that it is easier to obtain smooth results if the cornmeal is first soaked in cool liquid before combining it with hot liquid. The proportions vary slightly for each grind of cornmeal: For fine-grind cornmeal use 1 cup cornmeal to 3 cups liquid; for medium-grind 1 cup cornmeal to 3½ cups liquid; and for coarse grind 1 cup cornmeal to 4 cups of liquid. Imported Italian cornmeal requires a little extra liquid. Instant polenta is never to be used.

Here is the basic cooking method, using medium-grind cornmeal, which most resembles the Italian grind.

BASIC POLENTA

SERVES 4

1 cup medium-grind cornmeal

2½ cups tepid water

1 cup chicken broth (page 64) or meat broth (page 65) or good-quality store-bought

Salt and pepper

Put the cornmeal in a bowl and mix in 1 cup of the water. Bring the remaining water and broth to a boil in a 2-quart pot. When the water is at a rolling boil, stir in the cornmeal. Return the mixture to a boil and lower the heat to a simmer. Stir to the bottom of the pot occasionally to prevent the polenta from sticking. The polenta is ready when it falls away from the sides of the pot, about 15 minutes. Taste it to be sure—if it still is raw, it will feel sticky, and the grains will be hard. Season the polenta with the salt and pepper to taste.

Polenta may be prepared 1 or 2 hours before serving. Simply remove the pot from the heat and let it rest, covered, before reheating. If it becomes too firm or dry, add a little warm water. Medium-grind cornmeal makes an excellent firm polenta, ideal for most polenta dishes. Finely ground cornmeal is preferred for a soft polenta, and the coarse-grind is favored for grilled polenta. Fried and baked polenta dishes are made with polenta that has been refrigerated at least a few hours and up to a day or so. Cornmeal for polenta may be purchased in most Italian food stores, gourmet food shops, or health food stores.

POLENTA CON RAGÙ AL FORNO

⟨⟨⟨⟨⟨⟨⟨⟨

*BAKED POLENTA
WITH RAGÙ*

SERVES 4

2 recipes polenta, made with medium-grind cornmeal
½ cup freshly grated Parmigiano-Reggiano or more to taste
2 ounces Fontina or Münster, thinly sliced or shaved
2 to 2½ cups *Ragù di Parma* (page 62)

Preheat the oven to 350° F.

Pour half of the hot polenta onto an ovenproof platter or into a shallow baking dish. Cover the polenta with ¼ cup of the Parmigiano and all of the Fontina. Carefully pour the remaining polenta over the cheeses, cover it with the *ragù* and the remaining Parmigiano, and bake in the oven for about 15 minutes, or until the cheese begins to brown.

POLENTA SEMPLICE DI PARMA

⟨⟨⟨⟨⟨⟨⟨⟨

*PARMA'S BASIC
POLENTA*

SERVES 4

2 recipes polenta, made with medium-grind cornmeal
¼ cup butter
⅔ cup freshly grated Parmigiano-Reggiano

Pour the hot polenta onto a clean wooden board or serving platter. Dot the butter on the polenta to melt and sprinkle with ⅓ cup of the cheese. Serve the polenta at once, passing the remaining cheese at the table.

Variation: *Polenta di Farfanaro* (Apennine Farfanaro Polenta)

Omit the butter. Ladle a light layer of *Salsa di Pomodoro e Funghi* (page 59) over the polenta, and sprinkle with ¼ cup of the cheese. Serve the polenta at once, passing the remaining cheese at the table.

BASIC RISOTTO

*E*ndless risotto dishes are prepared according to a more or less basic method. It was that traditional method that my mentors taught me. First the rice is sautéed, with a flavoring agent such as onion or scallion, to loosen the starch from the surface of the grain; then some wine may be added and reduced until it is all but evaporated. Next, hot liquid—usually broth—is gradually added, about ½ cup at a time. The rice is stirred almost constantly as more liquid is added and absorbed, until the rice is tender but still slightly firm to the bite—*al dente*—and the overall texture is creamy but not soupy.

Even in our high-tech times, few adjustments to save time and energy can be made, because the process itself is critical to the quality of the dish. However, years ago at my father's restaurant, Camillo (where risotto was one of the signature dishes), I observed a small variation that can reduce the effort somewhat. It is the method I use today. The main departure from the traditional method is that half the broth is added at once and the rice is covered. Another is that I find it unnecessary to warm the broth.

Ideally, risotto is cooked without interruption and served at once. However, if necessary, the rice can be cooked through the incorporation of the first half of the liquid. Remove the pot from the heat until you are ready to finish. Keep in mind that the rice will continue to cook until it reaches room temperature, so the amount of liquid required to finish may vary.

Risotto that accompanies a braised entrée that has its own sauce is generally made a bit drier than risotto that is served alone, as a first course, or with an entrée that is not sauced.

> 2 to 3 teaspoons butter, oil, or a combination
> ¼ cup minced onion or scallions
> I cup Italian rice
> 3 1/2 to 4½ cups broth (page 64 or 65), or good-quality store-bought

Heat the butter in a medium-sized heavy pot. Add the onion and sauté until opaque but not browned; add the rice and continue to cook until the rice is translucent, about 30 seconds.

(continued)

Add half the broth and cover the pot. Cook, covered, over a low boil for 7 or 8 minutes, until the broth is absorbed; stir once or twice to keep the rice from sticking, but otherwise keep the pot covered. Add half the remaining broth and cook the rice, uncovered, stirring occasionally, until the liquid is absorbed.

Add the remaining broth and follow the same procedure. The finished risotto should be creamy and *al dente*; if it is not, add a small additional amount of broth and cook a few moments longer.

RISOTTO AL VIN ROSSO

Risotto with Red Wine

SERVES 6

This is excellent with entrées cooked in red wine. We always serve it with *Bistecca Fritta al Vin Rosso.*

¼ ounce dried *porcini* mushrooms

½ cup dry red wine

4 tablespoons butter

I medium onion, chopped

2 cups Italian rice

4 to 5 cups meat broth (page 65) or good-quality store-bought

½ cup freshly grated Parmigiano-Reggiano

Salt and pepper

Soak the mushrooms in the wine to soften. Heat the butter in a 4-quart saucepan or heavy pot over medium heat and add the onion. Drain the softened mushrooms, squeezing to extract as much of the liquid as possible, and reserve the soaking liquid. Chop the mushrooms, add them to the pan, and stir to prevent burning. When the onions are glazed and begin to soften, stir in the rice and sauté until it is translucent, stirring occasionally. (Italian rice will have a white dot in the middle of each grain). Add the reserved soaking liquid, bring it to a boil, and reduce by half. Add about 2½ cups of broth, lower the heat, and cook, covered, at a slow boil, stirring occasionally. When all the liquid is absorbed, add about 1¼ cups more broth and cook at a slow boil, uncovered, stirring occasionally. Repeat the procedure with the remaining broth until the risotto is *al dente* with a creamy texture. Add ¼ cup of the cheese to the risotto and season with salt and pepper to taste. Serve the risotto at once, passing the remaining cheese at the table.

FUNGHI SECCHI
Dried Mushrooms

Parma's food heritage includes the legendary mushrooms from Borgo Val di Taro. During the height of Val Taro's *porcini* season, everyone picks mushrooms. There are far too many for fresh consumption, so the excess are dried. Some people pick and dry mushrooms for home use, and others sell what they gather to a drying factory. Ambitious mushroom-pickers sell their dried mushrooms at the market, and there are those who sell their dried mushrooms in Piacenza, Parma, and Genoa, where merchants pack them for export.

I am quite fortunate in that I have never had to buy a dried mushroom. Thanks to friends and relatives, I have a constant supply. Kept moisture-free and air-tight, dried mushrooms will last a long time—perhaps up to twelve months. The small packages of dried mushrooms found in most stores are enough for two to four recipes.

Proper handling of dried mushrooms is simple but very important. They are reconstituted in tepid—room temperature—liquid. The liquid and the mushrooms may be added to the dish together, or the mushrooms may be squeezed to extract as much excess liquid as possible, reserving the liquid, and sautéed on their own.

It is important that the liquid in which dried mushrooms are soaked be no warmer than tepid or the mushrooms will lose their taste and be about as flavorful as a used tea bag. The reserved liquid can be used as well.

Risotto con Ragù della Val Taro

*Risotto with
Meat Sauce Val
Taro*

Serves 6

We always prepare this risotto as a *primo piatto* before *Petto di Vitello Ripieno di Camillo* (page 90). It canalso be served as an entrée for a simple meal, followed by a green salad.

4 to 6 tablespoons butter
½ medium onion, finely chopped
2 cups Italian rice
3 to 4 cups meat broth (page 65) or good-quality store-bought
1½ to 2 cups *Ragù della Val Taro* (page 61)
½ cup freshly grated Parmigiano-Reggiano
Salt and pepper

Heat the butter in a heavy pot and add the onion. When the onions are glazed and begin to soften, stir in the rice and sauté until it is translucent, stirring occasionally. Add about 2 cups of broth and cook the risotto, covered, at a slow boil, stirring occasionally. When the broth is absorbed, in about 7 minutes, add I cup of remaining broth and I cup of *ragù*. If necessary, repeat procedure with remaining sauce and broth. Simmer, uncovered, until risotto is *al dente* with a creamy texture. Add ¼ cup of the cheese to the risotto and season with salt and pepper to taste. Serve the risotto at once, passing the remaining cheese at the table.

Risotto allo Zafferano

Saffron Risotto

Serves 6

This risotto has a little more gusto than *risotto alla milanese*, which is also made with saffron. As in Milan, it is the one we serve with *osso buco*.

½ ounce dried *porcini* mushrooms
4 to 5 cups tepid meat broth (page 65) or good-quality store-bought
4 tablespoons butter
2 whole scallions, trimmed
¾ ounce prosciutto
2 cups Italian rice
⅛ teaspoon saffron threads
½ cup freshly grated Parmigiano-Reggiano
Salt and pepper

Soak the mushrooms in ½ cup of tepid broth to soften. Heat the butter in a heavy pot. Chop the scallions and prosciutto together and add them to the pot. Drain the softened mushrooms, squeezing to extract as much of the liquid as possible, and reserve the soaking liquid. Chop the mushrooms and add them to the pot. When the vegetables are soft and glazed, stir in the rice, sauté until it is translucent, and stir in the saffron. Add about 2 cups of broth and the reserved soaking liquid. Cook the risotto, covered, at a medium boil, for 8 to 10 minutes, stirring occasionally. When the broth is absorbed, add about 1¼ cups of broth and cook, uncovered, stirring occasionally. Repeat the procedure with the remaining broth until the rice is *al dente* with a creamy texture. Add a little more broth if the risotto seems dry. Season the risotto with the salt and pepper to taste. Remove the pot from the heat and stir 2 tablespoons of the cheese into the risotto. Serve the risotto at once, passing the remaining cheese at the table.

When serving this risotto with *osso buco*, arrange the shanks in the middle of a serving platter, surround them with the risotto, and pour some of the *osso buco* braising sauce over all.

RISOTTO PER POLLAME

RISOTTO FOR POULTRY

SERVES 6

*T*he combination of mushrooms and chicken seems to be successful in any manifestation. Here, dried mushrooms and chicken broth—try to use homemade for this—get added interest from the chicken liver. This is ideal with poultry dishes such as roast capon.

¼ ounce dried *porcini* mushrooms
I cup dry white wine
6 tablespoons butter
I chicken liver, chopped
I medium onion, chopped
2 whole scallions, thinly sliced
2 cups Italian rice
4 to 5 cups chicken broth (page 64) or good-quality store-bought
½ cup freshly grated Parmigiano-Reggiano
Salt and pepper

Soak the mushrooms in the wine to soften. Heat the butter in a 4-quart saucepan or heavy pot and add the chicken liver, onion, and scallions. Drain the softened mushrooms, squeezing to extract as much of the liquid as possible, and reserve the soaking liquid. Chop the mushrooms, and add them to the pan. When the onions are glazed and the livers are cooked until they are no longer pink, stir in the rice and sauté until translucent, stirring occasionally. Stir in the reserved soaking liquid, and cook the risotto at a medium boil for about 2 minutes, or until the liquid is reduced by half. Add about 2½ cups of broth and cook, covered, at a low boil until the broth is absorbed. Add about 1¼ cups of broth and cook, uncovered, stirring occasionally. Repeat the procedure with the remaining broth until the risotto is *al dente* with a creamy texture. Season the risotto with the salt and pepper to taste. Remove the pan from the heat and stir in 2 tablespoons of the cheese. Serve the risotto at once, passing the remaining cheese at the table.

RISOTTO ROBUSTO

Robust Risotto

SERVES 6

*T*his risotto preparation is excellent with hearty main courses; for me, it is a must with roast leg of lamb. As a *primo piatto* it teases the palate for the entrée.

¾ ounce dried *porcini* mushrooms

4 to 5 cups tepid meat broth (page 65) or good-quality store-bought

4 tablespoons butter

½ ounce prosciutto or *pancetta*, minced

I small onion

I rib celery

I clove finely chopped garlic

I teaspoon dried basil

2 cups Italian rice

½ cup chopped fresh tomatoes or canned crushed tomatoes, including the juice

4 tablespoons freshly grated Parmigiano-Reggiano

Salt and pepper

Soak the mushrooms in ½ cup tepid broth to soften. Heat the butter in a 4-quart saucepan or heavy pot and add the prosciutto. Drain the mushrooms, reserving the liquid, and squeeze dry of any excess liquid. Chop the mushrooms, onion, and celery and add them to the pan. Sauté the vegetables until they begin to soften but not brown, then add the garlic and basil. Stir in the rice and sauté, stirring occasionally, until translucent. Stir in the tomatoes with their juice and cook over medium heat for 2 minutes. Add the reserved soaking liquid and about 2½ cups of broth and cook the risotto, covered, at a slow boil until the liquid is absorbed, stirring occasionally. Add about 1¼ cups of broth and cook, uncovered, stirring occasionally. Repeat the procedure with the remaining broth until the risotto is *al dente* with a creamy texture. Season the risotto with the salt and pepper to taste. Remove the pan from the heat and stir in 2 tablespoons of the cheese. Serve the risotto at once, passing the remaining cheese at the table.

Risotto al Vin Bianco e Piselli

RISOTTO WITH
WHITE WINE
AND PEAS

SERVES 4

*T*his is excellent with delicate main courses, particularly fish dishes. The wine seems to intensify the sweetness of the peas. If they are in season, fresh peas are well worth the extra effort here.

¼ ounce dried *porcini* mushrooms

½ cup dry white wine

3 tablespoons butter

½ medium onion, chopped

1 cup Italian rice

2½ to 3½ cups chicken broth (page 64) or good-quality store-bought

½ cup new peas (fresh or frozen)

Salt and pepper

¼ cup freshly grated Parmigiano-Reggiano

Soak the mushrooms in the wine to soften. Heat the butter in a 4-quart saucepan or heavy pot and sauté the onions until soft. Stir in the rice and sauté until translucent. Add the mushrooms and wine and let the wine sizzle about 20 seconds. Add about 2 cups of broth and simmer the risotto, covered, stirring occasionally, until most of the broth is absorbed, about 10 minutes. Add about 1 cup of broth and cook, uncovered, at a medium boil. Repeat the procedure with the remaining broth until the risotto is *al dente* with a creamy texture. Season the risotto to taste with the salt and pepper. Remove the pan from the heat and stir in 1½ to 2 tablespoons of the cheese. Serve the risotto at once, passing the remaining cheese at the table.

38 THE COOKING OF PARMA

PASTA FRESCA

*O*ur basic fresh pasta dough is used to make *farfallette*—little bow ties—and *tagliatelle*—long noodles—as well as the famed filled pastas of Parma. Italian cooks begin by placing the flour on a pastry board and whipping some of the liquid into the flour with a fork; they then continue the process with their hands. I use a bowl because I do not want flour all over the kitchen, and I use my hands for the entire process. The amount of flour that will be incorporated will vary with the humidity.

> 3½ cups flour
> 3 extra-large eggs
> ½ cup water
> ½ teaspoon salt

Put the flour in a large mixing bowl. Make a well in the middle of the flour and put the remaining ingredients into it. Using a fork, whip a bit of the flour into the liquid. Continue to incorporate the flour into the liquid, using your hands, until a ball can be formed, then turn the mixture out onto a pastry board. The ball should be just damp to the touch, not sticky or dry. If it is too dry, add I or 2 more tablespoons of water; if too sticky, spread a little flour on the pastry board and knead it in. Knead the dough for about 10 minutes, or until it is smooth, elastic, and barely damp to the touch.

The dough is now ready to be rolled, cut, and shaped as needed. Always cook pasta in boiling water to which salt has been added just before the pasta, and never add oil to the water.

PASTA VERDE

Spinach Pasta

Green pasta was developed by poor cooks when there were not enough vegetables to go around. Whatever greens were available were incorporated into pasta dough as a way of distributing nutrients to everyone.

½ pound fresh spinach or ½ package (5 ounces) frozen spinach
2¼ cups flour
½ teaspoon salt
2 eggs
3 tablespoons water

Cook the spinach, squeeze out as much water as possible, and chop finely. Put 2 cups of the flour in a large mixing bowl, make a well and add the spinach and the remaining ingredients. Make the pasta according to the method for *Pasta Fresca*, (page 39).

If you are using a pasta machine, feed the dough through the rollers set on the widest notch and progress to the next to the last notch. Using the wide noodle attachment, cut the dough into *tagliatelle*.

To make noodles by hand, roll out the dough thinly to a rectangle about 22 by 24 inches. Sprinkle the dough with flour and roll up the sheet of pasta loosely. Cut along the pasta roll at ¼-inch intervals and unroll the noodles.

TAGLIATELLE VERDI CON PARMIGIANO

SPINACH PASTA WITH CHEESE

SERVES 4 AS A FIRST COURSE

½ recipe *Pasta Verde* (page 40)

4 to 6 tablespoons butter

Salt and pepper

¼ cup freshly grated Parmigiano-Reggiano

Bring a pot of water to a rolling boil and add a pinch of salt. Add the noodles and cook carefully until they are just al dente. Drain the noodles in a colander. Return the pot to the stove over medium heat and add the butter. When it is melted, return the noodles to the pot. Mix the noodles gently, remove the pot from the heat and season with salt and pepper to taste. Gently stir in the cheese. Serve the noodles at once.

ANOLINI AND ANULIN

Anolini, small (1¼ inch in diameter), round, filled pasta pillows are the gastronomic pride and joy of Parma. It is said that the aristocrats of what now is Parma have been feasting on these delicate treats—called *anolen* in the Parmesan dialect—for about 1500 years. *Anolini* are defined by three ingredients: beef, Parmigiano-Reggiano, and nutmeg in the filling. Other ingredients, such as carrots or onions, may be part of a cook's interpretation, but lacking one of the critical three, the stuffed pasta at hand cannot be called *anolini*. Almost invariably, *anolini* are served in meat or chicken broth. *Anolini* are not to be confused with Bologna's *tortellini*, or any other pasta.

Travel west of the city and in thirty minutes the road begins to twist and turn through the province's Apennine Mountains, to the center, Val Taro–Val Ceno. Here the filled pasta served in broth is a touch smaller (¾ inch to 1 inch in diameter) and half-moon shaped. Known as *anulin*, the filling is lighter in color from pale-colored meats such as chicken, pigeon, wild boar combined with pigeon, pheasant, or pork. Today, pork and chicken is a popular combination, while nutmeg is rarely included.

ANOLINI DI PARMA

PARMA'S ANOLINI

SERVES 10

2 tablespoons butter

1 medium onion, chopped

3 cloves garlic, finely minced

3 thin slices prosciutto, chopped

½ pound beef from *Stracotto di Manzo* (page 83)

½ cup dry red wine

1¼ cups meat essence from the *Stracotto* (page 83)

1 teaspoon freshly grated nutmeg

½ cup ricotta

3 tablespoons chopped fresh parsley

2 eggs

½ cup freshly grated Parmigiano-Reggiano

1 recipe *Pasta Fresca* (page 39)

3 quarts meat broth (page 65) or good-quality store-bought

Heat the butter in a sauté pan and sauté the onion, garlic, and prosciutto over low heat. Dice the pot roast, add it to the pan, and cook until all ingredients are well blended. Add the wine and boil for 1 minute, or until it is reduced by half. Add the pot roast sauce and simmer, covered, until the meat begins to fall apart, about 30 minutes.

Remove the pan from the heat and let the mixture cool until it can be handled. Finely chop the mixture using a meat grinder or food processor, but do not overprocess or purée. Add the nutmeg, ricotta, parsley, 1 egg, and cheese and mix well.

Make an egg wash by beating together the remaining egg and 2 teaspoons of water in a dish.

Roll out the pasta dough as thinly and as square as possible, about 24 by 27 inches. Starting from the bottom and on ½ of the sheet of dough only, put ½ rounded teaspoons of filling in rows, about 1½ inches apart (a pastry bag can be used). Using a small brush, paint around each filling. Carefully fold the other side of dough over to cover the fillings, pressing the edges together to seal them well. Use an *anolini* cutter, biscuit cutter, or glass to cut out disks about 1¼ inch in diameter. Gather up the excess dough and repeat the procedure until all the dough is used. The excess filling can be used for *Uccelii di Vitello* (page 97).

If the pasta is rolled out with a pasta machine, put the filling in 2 rows along the length of 1 sheet of dough, paint the egg wash around the filling and cover with another dough sheet. Paint around the fillings, pressing to seal, and cut out disks as above.

Bring 4 quarts of lightly salted water to a boil in a pot, and bring the broth to a simmer in another pot. Carefully drop the *anolini* into the boiling water. When they rise to the surface, transfer them with a strainer to the broth and cook them until *al dente*, about 8 minutes.

ANULIN

**APENNINE
MOUNTAIN-STYLE
FILLED PASTA
IN BROTH**

SERVES 10

*A*hen that is too old to provide eggs is the basis for chicken broth. The cooked chicken is used in the filling for the pasta, and the *anulin* are served in the broth. By serving chicken-filled *anulin* in chicken broth, a richer, more intense blend of flavors is obtained.

4 tablespoons butter

½ medium onion, chopped

I scallion, trimmed and thinly sliced

I recipe chicken broth (page 64)

½ pound boneless chicken meat from the broth

I onion from the broth, chopped

I celery rib from the broth, chopped

4 ounces very fresh *mascarpone* or other soft cheese such as cream cheese

½ cup freshly grated Parmigiano-Reggiano

2 tablespoons chopped fresh parsley

2 eggs

Salt and pepper

I recipe *Pasta Fresca* (page 39)

Heat the butter in a sauté pan and carefully sauté the onion and scallion over medium heat until the onion is soft and translucent. Add the chicken, onion, and celery from the broth and sauté for 2 minutes. Add ¼ cup broth and cook, covered, over medium heat for 10 minutes. Remove the pan from the heat and let the mixture cool until it can be handled. Finely chop the mixture using a meat grinder or food processor, but do not overprocess or purée. Mix in the cheeses, parsley, I egg, and salt and pepper to taste.

Make an egg wash by beating together the remaining egg and 2 teaspoons of water in a small dish.

Roll out the dough as thin as possible (paper thin), about 24 by 27 inches. One inch from the bottom, drop ½ teaspoons of filling (a pastry bag can be used) I inch apart from I end of the dough to the other end. With the egg wash paint all around the mounds of filling. Seal the dough on each side of the filling. With a small round cookie cutter, cut between the mounds of filling (do not cut along the folded edge) to form half-moon shapes. Cut off the jagged edge, gather up the excess dough, and repeat the procedure until all the dough is used.

If the pasta is rolled out with a pasta machine, put the filling in 1 row along the center of the dough. Paint the egg wash around the filling and fold the dough lengthwise, pressing to seal. Cut into half moons (do not cut along the folded edge).

Bring 4 quarts of lightly salted water to a boil in a pot and bring the broth to a simmer in another pot. Carefully drop the *anulin* into the boiling water. When they rise to the surface, transfer them with a strainer to the broth and cook until they are *al dente*, about 8 minutes.

Roll out the pasta dough about 24 inches by 27 inches (it should be paper thin). Draw an imaginary line across the middle of the rolled-out dough. On the imaginary line, ½ inch from the edge, put 1½-teaspoon mounds of filling 1 inch apart, until you reach the other edge. Begin another line of filling 1 inch below the first and continue until half the sheet of dough is filled. Make an egg wash by beating 1 egg yolk with about 1 tablespoon water and, using a small brush, paint the dough between each filling. Carefully fold the unpainted dough over the filling.

Flour an edge of a cutting board that is about 15 inches long with edges that are about ¾ inch thick and press the floured edge between each filling to seal well. Using a zigzag pasta cutter, cut between each filling. Alternatively, follow the instructions for forming *anolini*, using a zigzag cutter.

TORTELLI DI ZUCCA

RAVIOLI WITH WINTER SQUASH

MAKES ABOUT 75 TORTELLI, SERVES 6 AS AN ENTRÉE

*Z*ucca is an Italian squash not found here—it seems to be incapable of being transplanted. The American pumpkin or butternut squash are excellent alternatives. My first choice is pumpkin. I generally serve these tortelli with a little butter and just a splash of milk, but they also can be served with butter and cheese.

FOR THE TORTELLI:

    1 recipe *Pasta Fresca* (page 39)
    2 pounds pumpkin or butternut squash
    3 tablespoons butter
    ¼ cup chopped chives or scallions
    2 tablespoons chopped fresh parsley
    ½ teaspoon freshly grated nutmeg
    4 ounces very fresh *mascarpone* or other soft cheese such as cream cheese
    ½ cup freshly grated Parmigiano-Reggiano
    1 egg

6 tablespoons butter
½ cup milk
½ cup freshly grated Parmigiano-Reggiano
Salt and pepper

Preheat oven to 375° F.

Cut the pumpkin in half, prick the shell all over, and place it, flesh down, on a baking sheet. Bake until tender. When the pumpkin is cool enough to handle, peel and seed it and pass it through a ricer into a mixing bowl (do not purée). Heat the butter in a sauté pan and sauté the chives until soft. Add the parsley, nutmeg, cheeses, and 1 egg and mix well.

To form the *tortelli*, see the box on page 46. If you are using a pasta machine, make 2 rows of filling along each strip and follow the instructions above. If you are using ravioli forms, follow the manufacturer's instructions.

Bring 4 quarts of water to a boil in a pot and add a pinch of salt. Drop in the *tortelli* and cook until *al dente*, 6 to 7 minutes. Drain the *tortelli* in a colander.

To make the sauce: Return the pot to the stove over medium heat and add the butter. When it is melted, return the *tortelli* to the pot. Add the milk, bring it to a boil, and gently mix. Remove the pot from the heat, gently mix in ¼ cup of the cheese, and season with salt and pepper to taste. Pass the remaining cheese at the table.

OVERLEAF, CLOCKWISE
FROM TOP: *Risotto with White Wine and Peas, Cannelloni, Spinach Pasta, Gnocchi with Mushrooms, Pegai, Ravioli with Pot Roast and Spinach, Baked Polenta with Ragù*

POLENTA, RISOTTO, PASTA AND GNOCCHI

Ravioli di Brasato di Manzo e Spinaci

*P*arma's ravioli is filled with meat and spinach or another green. The meat and vegetables typically are what is left from *Brasato di Manzo* (page 84). A little cooked chicken, pork, or veal also can be added for a delicate touch.

4 tablespoons butter

I medium onion, chopped

I teaspoon dried basil

¼ teaspoon dried thyme

I bay leaf

½ pound beef from *Brasato di Manzo* (page 84)

½ cup chopped vegetables from *Brasato di Manzo* (page 84; optional)

¼ cup sauce from the *Brasato* plus additional if necessary

4 ounces cooked chopped spinach (about ¾ cup)

½ cup ricotta or ¼ cup very fresh *mascarpone* or other soft cheese

¼ cup freshly grated Parmigiano-Reggiano

I egg

Salt and pepper

I recipe *Pasta Fresca* (page 39)

Heat the butter in a sauté pan and add the onion. Cut the beef into pieces the size of walnuts and add them to the pan with the chopped cooked vegetables. Stir in the herbs and the meat sauce and simmer, covered, for 10 minutes. Add additional sauce if the mixture seems dry.

Remove the pan from the heat, and let the mixture cool until it can be handled. Finely chop the mixture using a meat grinder or food processor but do not overprocess or purée. Put the mixture in a bowl, add the chopped spinach, cheeses, I egg, and salt and pepper to taste and mix well.

To form the ravioli, see the box on page 46. If you are using a pasta machine, roll out strips of dough using the widest notch. Make 2 rows of filling along each strip and follow the instructions for forming ravioli.

Bring 4 quarts of water to a boil in a pot and add a pinch of salt. Drop in the ravioli and cook until tender. Drain the ravioli in a colander.

PEGAI

*T*he easiest to make filled pasta is found only in the Apennines. Originally a meatless Lenten dish, *pegai*, and a salad, is a fantastic meal any time. Aunt Irma always wondered why Nonna Vecchia never tasted the filling before cooking, so one time we did taste and discovered that *pegai* is a good example of how food changes chemically as it cooks. What is not so wonderful in its raw state develops magnificent tastes in the process.

FOR THE *PEGAI*:

> 1 pound chestnut flour
> 1⅓ to 1½ cups milk
> 3 tablespoons freshly grated Parmigiano-Reggiano
> Salt and pepper
> 1 recipe *Pasta Fresca* (page 39)

FOR THE SAUCE:

> 1 pound ricotta at room temperature
> 1⅓ cups milk at room temperature
> ½ cup chopped walnuts
> 2 tablespoons chopped parsley (optional)
> Salt and pepper
> Freshly grated Parmigiano-Reggiano

To make the *pegai*: Put the chestnut flour in a mixing bowl and slowly stir in the milk until the mixture is the consistency of peanut butter. Add the cheese and the salt and pepper to taste.

Roll out the pasta dough paper thin. Spread the chestnut filling on ½ of the sheet of dough and carefully fold the other half over the filling, gently pressing out any air. Cut into ½- by 1-inch diagonal rectangles. Although it seems as though the filling will slip out the cut edges, it will not.

To make the sauce: Put the ricotta in a large mixing bowl and whip in the milk. Mix in the walnuts and the salt and pepper to taste.

Bring 2½ quarts of water to a boil in a pot and add a pinch of salt. Drop in the *pegai* and cook them at a medium low boil for 8 minutes, or until they are *al dente*. Drain the pegai in a colander and add them to the sauce. Sprinkle with the parsley and pass the Parmigiano at the table.

TURTEI

*T*urtei is dialect for pasta filled with greens and herbs. In Italian it is *tortelli d'erbette* but the preparations are somewhat different so for accuracy we refer to Parma's version as *turtei*.

I learned the basics of this pasta after a meal of *pegai* at Nonno Conti's house. I mentioned to the family that I had eaten spinach-filled pasta. Nonno said, "*Turtei*—the secrets lie with some of us in the mountains."

Of course I asked how to prepare *turtei*. He said, 'You need three greens to do it correctly. Generally spinach, Swiss chard, and beet tops are used, but kale or another green can be used, depending on what's available." My mother added that just a little cream cheese and an egg are needed to smoothly tie everything together, with Parmigiano-Reggiano for flavor.

Today, there are other versions of pastas filled with greens. There is one kind filled with ricotta and a smidgen of greens. *Tortelli d'erbette* is about half greens and half cheese. Maybe when it all began there were more greens and less cheese in the Apennines.

There are three steps to preparing this pasta and they can be done over three days.

FOR THE *TURTEI*:

½ pound fresh spinach

½ pound fresh Swiss chard

½ pound fresh beet greens

3 tablespoons butter

⅓ cup sliced scallions

2 tablespoons chopped fresh basil or ½ teaspoon dried

¼ cup chopped fresh parsley

4 ounces very fresh *mascarpone* or other soft cheese such as cream cheese

½ cup freshly grated Parmigiano-Reggiano

I egg

Salt and pepper

I recipe *Pasta Fresca* (page 39)

> 6 tablespoons butter
> ½ cup freshly grated Parmigiano-Reggiano
> ½ cup milk
> Salt and pepper

Keeping them separate, trim the greens of their stems and tough ribs and discard any discolored or badly bruised leaves. Carefully wash the greens, changing the water once or twice as necessary. Steam the greens separately in pots filled with 3 inches of boiling salted water. Drain the greens in a colander and immediately chill under ice water to stop the cooking. Squeeze out as much liquid as possible and chop the greens.

Put the greens in a large mixing bowl. Melt the butter in a sauté pan, cook the scallions until very soft, but not browned, and add them to the greens. Add the herbs, cheese, egg, salt and pepper to taste and mix well.

To form the *turtei*, see the box on page 46. If you are using a pasta machine, roll out strips of dough using the widest notch. Make 2 rows of filling along each strip and follow the instructions above.

Cook the *turtei* in salted boiling water until *al dente*, 6 to 7 minutes.

In a serving dish, mix together the butter, cheese, a splash of milk, and the salt and pepper to taste. Drain the *turtei* in a colander, immediately turn them into the dish, and gently coat them with the sauce.

Note: Other light sauces, such as *Salsa di Pomodoro e Funghi* (page 59) and *Salsa di Funghi e Sugo* (page 60) also can be used with *turtei*.

CANNELLONI

▰▰▰▰▰▰▰▰

MAKES 12 CANNELLONI
SERVES 6

When my teenage sons returned from a holiday in Val Taro, they requested classic cannelloni prepared the way they enjoyed it in Val Taro. I know other people who will eat cannelloni only in the province of Parma. A veal filling is rolled in a crêpe and baked in a white sauce. I use the excess meat from *Vitello Arrosto con Verdure Miste* (page 92) or veal cooked for broth. A little chicken also can be included. This dish may be prepared in advance and baked the next day. The filled crêpes can be kept frozen for up to 9 weeks.

FOR THE FILLING:

¾ ounce dried *porcini* mushrooms

½ cup dry white wine

5 tablespoons butter

½ carrot (see note below)

I rib celery (see note below)

½ medium onion (see note below)

I whole scallion, sliced

I teaspoon dried basil

½ teaspoon freshly grated nutmeg

3 bay leaves

I½ to 2 pounds cooked veal

I pound ricotta

½ cup chopped fresh parsley

½ cup freshly grated Parmigiano-Reggiano

2 eggs

Salt and pepper

FOR THE CRÊPES:

I cup flour

I ¼ cups milk

¼ cup Marsala

2 eggs

2 tablespoons melted butter, cooled

¼ teaspoon salt

3 tablespoons vegetable oil

> see *Lasagne in Bianco* (page 58)
> Freshly grated Parmigiano-Reggiano

To make the filling: Soak the mushrooms in the wine to soften them. Heat the butter in a deep, heavy sauté pan. Cut the carrot, celery, and onion into small pieces and add them to the pan. When they are cooked, add the scallion. Drain the softened mushrooms, sqeezing to extract as much liquid as possible, and reserve the soaking liquid. Chop the mushrooms and add them to the pan. When all the flavors are blended, after 3 to 4 minutes, mix in the basil, nutmeg, bay leaves, and veal. Add the reserved soaking liquid and simmer, covered, for 5 minutes.

Remove the pan from the heat and let the mixture cool until it can be handled. Finely chop the mixture using a meat grinder or food processor but do not overprocess or purée. Mix in the ricotta, parsley, Parmigiano, eggs and salt and pepper to taste.

To make the crêpes: Put the flour in a mixing bowl and mix in the milk, wine, eggs, butter, and salt. Put 1 tablespoon of oil in a 6-inch sauté pan and drain off excess. (There should be a light coating of oil in the pan.) Heat the pan over medium heat and with a ladle, add 2 tablespoons of batter, tilting and turning the pan to distribute the batter evenly over the bottom. Cook the crêpe for about 30 seconds, or until golden brown on the bottom, and turn and brown on the other side. As the crêpes brown, transfer them to a plate, overlapping them. Add additional oil to the pan if necessary.

To make the sauce, follow the instructions on page 58.

Preheat the oven to 400° F.

Using your hands, mold the filling into cylinders 1 inch in diameter and 4 inches long. Wrap the crêpes around the cylinders. Put a little of the sauce on the bottom of a casserole dish about 9 by 6 inches. Arrange the cannelloni, seams down, in the dish, cover them with the remaining sauce, and sprinkle with a few tablespoons of Parmigiano. Bake the cannelloni in the oven for 35 to 40 minutes, or until lightly browned on top.

Note: If you are using leftover *Vitello Arrosto con Vedure Miste*, use some of the vegetables from that recipe.

GNOCCHI DI PATATE

Potato Gnocchi

SERVES 6

*G*nocchi are miniature dumplings usually included in the pasta category, though they are not truly pasta. In Parma *gnocchi* are made with potatoes. *Gnocchi* are served as an independent dish—as the pasta course—or as an accompaniment to an entrée. They are especially good with some of the braised meat dishes in this book.

I find the microwave oven a great aid in cooking the potatoes because it cooks them faster and the result is good. Simply puncture the potatoes with a fork, bake them on high power for about 7 minutes, turn them and bake for 7 more minutes. Some potatoes will need a little more time.

The Variation is a favorite of my wife, Betty. Our introduction to this dish was in Borgo Val di Taro during the height of the *porcini* mushroom season. Driving down the mountain and along the Taro River, the air was filled with the aroma of mushrooms popping through the soil. People were walking along the sides of the road with baskets of mushrooms. The sight of those basketsand the wonderful scent made it impossible to drive any farther without lunching on mushrooms. We feasted on *gnocchi con funghi*.

2 to 2¼ pounds russet potatoes, scrubbed but not peeled
2 cups flour plus additional if necessary
Salt and white pepper
1 extra-large egg

Boil, steam, bake, or microwave the potatoes. Let the potatoes cool until they can be handled and peel them. Pass the potatoes through a ricer onto a pastry board or table.

Sprinkle 2 cups of flour and the salt and pepper to taste over the potatoes. Beat the egg a bit and add it to the potato mixture. Mix the ingredients together until a ball is formed. If the dough is sticky, knead in additional flour. Knead the dough on a floured board for 5 minutes. The dough should be smooth, springy, and damp to the touch but not sticky.

On a floured board roll the dough into long cylinders about ¼ inch in diameter. Cut the cylinders into pieces ½ inch long. Sprinkle a tray with flour. Using your thumb, roll the pieces along the tines of a fork or against a cheese grater onto the tray.

Bring 3 quarts of salted water to a boil. Add the *gnocchi* to the boiling water and stir carefully with a wooden spoon. When the *gnocchi* rise to the surface, taste one—if it is light and just *al dente*, it is perfect. Drain the *gnocchi* in a colander and serve at once.

VARIATION: GNOCCHI DI PATATE CON FUNGHI

POTATO GNOCCHI
WITH MUSHROOMS

Heat 6 tablespoons butter in a saucepan, slice 8 ounces fresh or ½ cup dried *porcini* mushrooms, and sauté in the butter about 10 minutes. Add the *gnocchi* and salt and pepper to taste to the pan; remove the pan and add ¼ cup of Parmigiano.

If you use dried *porcini*, soak them in ½ cup of tepid water to soften. Drain, squeezing to extract as much of the liquid as possible, and reserve the soaking liquid. Add the mushrooms and liquid to the butter and sauté over medium-high heat to reduce most of the liquid.

GNOCCHI CON RAGÙ DI PARMA E LUGANEGA

GNOCCHI WITH
PARMA'S MEAT SAUCE
AND THIN SAUSAGE

SERVES 4 TO 6

With the light but substantial *gnocchi* and the tasty sausage this can be served as an entrée. It was a very popular luncheon dish at my father's restaurant, Camillo's.

> I pound *luganega* sausage (see note)
> I recipe *Gnocchi di Patate* (page 56)
> 3 cups *Ragù di Parma* (page 62)
> **Freshly grated Parmigiano-Reggiano**

Prick the *luganega* and sauté or grill it until it is browned and cooked through. Heat the *ragù*.

In a serving dish, combine the *ragù* and *gnocchi*. Arrange the *luganega* around the edges of the *gnocchi* and serve with the cheese.

Note: *Luganega* is a thin Italian pork sausage that can be found at Italian groceries or specialty food shops. If necessary sweet Italian or thin French sausage can be substituted.

LASAGNE IN BIANCO

◆◆◆◆◆◆◆◆◆◆

WHITE LASAGNE
SERVES 4

*M*ade without tomato sauce, meat or much cheese, the Parma style with this classic dish gives it a fresh perception.

I recipe *Pasta Fresca* (page 39)
½ cup butter
½ medium onion, sliced
I cup flour
½ teaspoon freshly grated nutmeg
3½ cups milk
½ cup chicken broth (page 64) or good-quality store-bought
2 eggs
½ cup Marsala
1½ cups freshly grated Parmigiano-Reggiano
Salt and pepper

Roll out the pasta dough to the thickness of 3 sheets of paper and cut into strips 3½ by 12 inches. Cook the pasta in 4 quarts of salted boiling water until almost *al dente*.

Preheat the oven to 400°F.

Heat the butter in a 3-quart pot and cook the onion until tender. Remove the onion from the butter with a slotted spoon. Mix the flour into the butter and cook, stirring, over low heat for 3 minutes or so. Add the nutmeg, slowly mix in the milk, and cook at a low simmer, stirring, until the sauce can thickly coat the back of a spoon. Stir in the broth and bring the mixture just to a simmer. Cook the mixture until it lightly coats the back of a spoon and remove the pot from the heat. When the sauce has cooled so that it is just warm to the touch, add the eggs, Marsala, about ⅓ cup of the cheese, and the salt and pepper to taste and whip until smooth.

Put a shallow layer of sauce (⅓ to ½ cup) in the bottom of a 9- by 6- by 2-inch baking dish and cover with strips of pasta. Ladle 1½ cups of sauce over and sprinkle evenly with some remaining cheese. Top with another layer of pasta and repeat until all the ingredients have been used. Bake for about 45 minutes, or until the top is slightly golden brown.

Note: The lasagne may be assembled I day in advance.

SAUCES

SALSA DI POMODORO E FUNGHI

*TOMATO MUSHROOM
SAUCE*
SERVES 6

*T*his easy sauce takes 30 to 40 minutes to prepare and is excellent with ravioli, polenta, or *gnocchi*.

4 tablespoons olive oil

8 ounces cleaned sliced fresh mushrooms

1 small onion, chopped

1 clove garlic, chopped

2 teaspoons dried basil

2 (28-ounce) cans whole tomatoes with juice

¼ cup chopped fresh parsley

Salt and pepper

Heat the oil in a saucepan, sauté the mushrooms for 3 to 4 minutes, and add the onion and garlic. When the onion is soft and translucent, stir in the basil and cook about 1 minute.

Break the tomatoes into pieces, add them with their liquid and the salt and pepper to taste to the pan, and simmer for 30 minutes.

SALSA DI FUNGHI E SUGO

MUSHROOM SAUCE WITH A HINT OF MEAT ESSENCE

SERVES 6

*T*his is a tasty, quick and easy sauce that is very good with ravioli and excellent with polenta, *gnocchi*, or *turtei*.

8 tablespoons butter
10 ounces cleaned sliced fresh mushrooms
¼ cup meat essence from a roast or pot roast
1 tablespoon chopped fresh parsley
Salt and pepper

Heat the butter in a sauté pan and sauté the mushrooms until they brown slightly. Add the meat essence and cook the mushrooms, covered, until tender, about 10 minutes. Add the parsley and salt and pepper to taste.

ABOUT RAGÙ

Ragù is at the heart of the cuisine of the region of Emilia-Romagna, particularly Emilia. Each province, indeed, each town has its own *ragù*. The most famous meat sauce of all is probably *Ragù alla Bolognese*, or Bolognese sauce. Of course, we Parmesans have our own version. Actually, we have two versions, one that is typical of the city of Parma, the other from the Apennines of Val Taro.

I first learned of *ragù di Parma* as an apprentice at my father's restaurant, Camillo. There the *ragù* was based on coarsely ground or diced veal. Val Taro's *ragù*, made with finely chopped meat, is the lightest. Country circumstances may dictate the meat used—if a cow stops giving milk, it may be beef; if a hunter is successful, venison or wild boar; veal is still another possibility.

Today it is mostly a matter of personal taste—some people prefer beef, while my family prefers a combination of veal, beef, and pork. Venison and wild boar may be hard to come by, but they make excellent traditional versions, particularly venison. I prepare venison *ragù* with spinach *farfalette* for the local hunters.

Ragù della Val Taro

**Val Taro's
Meat Sauce**

SERVES 8 AS A
SIDE DISH OR AS
A *PRIMO PIATTO*

*M*y mother, my aunts, and my grandparents all made this *ragù*—it was one of the constants of my family's table.

½ ounce dried *porcini* mushrooms

1 cup dry red wine

2 tablespoons olive oil

1 celery rib, chopped

½ medium onion, chopped

1 to 1¼ pounds chopped meat (⅓ veal, ⅓ beef, ⅓ pork or venison)

1 large clove garlic, chopped

2 tablespoons dried basil

1 teaspoon dried thyme

2 or 3 bay leaves

1 cup meat broth (page 65) or good-quality store-bought

2 (28-ounce) cans crushed tomatoes

Salt and pepper

Soak the mushrooms in the wine to soften them. Heat the oil in a saucepan over medium heat and add the celery and onion. Put the meat over the vegetables and sprinkle the garlic over all. As the vegetables and meat begin to brown, stir the mixture occasionally. When the meat is well-browned, add the herbs and the mushrooms with their soaking liquid, bring the mixture to a medium boil, and reduce the liquid by half. Add the broth, return the mixture to a medium boil, and reduce again by half. Add the tomatoes and the salt and pepper to taste, bring the mixture to a simmer, and simmer, covered, for 30 to 35 minutes, stirring occasionally.

RAGÙ DI PARMA

*A*t my father's restaurant, Camillo, this *ragù* was prepared for specialty items, such as *gnocchi*, ravioli, and polenta.

½ ounce dried *porcini* mushrooms

½ cup dry white wine

3 tablespoons olive oil

2 ounces coarsely chopped *pancetta* or prosciutto

I carrot, chopped

I celery rib, chopped

I medium onion, chopped

I¼ pound coarsely ground or diced veal (see note below)

I clove garlic, minced

I teaspoon freshly grated nutmeg

2 tablespoons flour

I½ cups meat broth (page 65) or good-qualtiy store-bought

2 fresh plum tomatoes, chopped

Salt and pepper

Soak the mushrooms in the wine to soften them. Heat the oil in a heavy saucepan and add the *pancetta*, carrot, celery, and onion. Put the veal over the vegetables to begin browning. After 4 or 5 minutes, stir the veal into the vegetables and add the garlic and nutmeg.

Drain the softened mushrooms, squeezing to extract as much liquid as possible, and reserve soaking liquid. Chop the mushrooms and stir them into the vegetable and meat mixture. When the meat is well-browned, mix in the flour. Add the reserved soaking liquid and simmer for 5 minutes. Add the broth and simmer, covered, until the veal is tender, 40 to 50 minutes. Add the tomatoes and the salt and pepper to taste and cook, uncovered, for about 15 minutes, or until the liquid is reduced to cover the meat by ¼ inch.

Note: Ask the butcher to grind the veal using a ¼-inch blade. You can also cut the veal into ¼-inch dice by hand or pass it through a meat grinder with a ¼-inch blade.

Minestre
and Zuppe

BRODO DI POLLO

CHICKEN BROTH

It may take several hours for a good broth to be made, but the actual hands-on time is a matter of minutes. You can listen to your favorite opera while the fragrant and flavorful concoction develops. The cooked chicken can be used to fill various pastas such as the *anulin* on page 44, served with vegetables, with *salsa verde* (page 111), vinaigrette (page 21), or *mostarda di frutta* (Note, page 111). Turkey can also be substituted as long as its distinctive flavor will not compromise the finished dish, but a mature full-grown chicken is best. Every part of the chicken can be included except the liver. When only bones are available, less water is used because the flavor will not be very intense.

> A 4-pound chicken, washed and liver reserved for another use
> 4 carrots, trimmed and washed but not peeled
> 4 large celery ribs, trimmed and washed
> 4 onions, wiped clean and stem removed
> 1 clove garlic, crushed and peeled
> 2 bay leaves
> 4 sprigs parsley, washed
> ½ teaspoon whole peppercorns
> Salt

Put all the ingredients except the salt into a large soup pot, add four quarts water, and bring just to a simmer over medium heat. Immediately lower the heat (do not allow the broth to boil) and maintain a low simmer until the chicken is tender, about 3 hours. Add the salt to taste.

Remove the pot from the heat, and let cool, uncovered, to room temperature. Remove the chicken and the vegetables from the broth, strain the broth through a fine sieve or cheesecloth into a bowl and refrigerate. This will allow the fat to rise to the top and solidify, and the impurities will settle to the bottom. Before using, skim the fat from the top and carefully remove the broth from the bowl without disturbing the impurities. The broth may be prepared in advance and stored in the refrigerator for up to 1 week or in the freezer for up to 6 weeks.

BRODO DI CARNE

MEAT BROTH

This broth is an excellent all-purpose base. Again, the use of an older chicken is recommended, and the soup bones are best if they have a little meat on them. This recipe is a case where I sometimes use only the chicken carcass, meat bones, and half the usual amount of water.

> A 2½-pound chicken, washed and liver reserved for another use
> 2 pounds veal soup bones
> 2 pounds beef soup bones
> 4 carrots, trimmed and washed but not peeled
> 4 celery ribs, trimmed and washed
> 4 medium onions, wiped clean and stem removed
> 1 clove garlic, peeled and cut in half
> 2 or 3 bay leaves
> 3 sprigs parsley, washed
> ½ to ⅓ cup roughly chopped leeks
> Salt and pepper

Put all the ingredients except the salt and pepper in a large soup pot, add four quarts water, and bring just to a simmer over medium heat, skimming the foam. Maintain broth at a low simmer for 2 to 3 hours (do not let the broth boil). When the meat is well cooked and has given up all its juices, remove it from the pot and continue to simmer the bones and broth for 1 more hour. Season the broth to taste with the salt and pepper and simmer 10 more minutes, skimming the foam.

Remove the pot from the heat and let cool, uncovered, to room temperature. Strain the broth through a sieve or cheesecloth into a bowl and refrigerate. The fat will rise to the top and solidify, and the impurities will settle to the bottom. Before using, remove the fat from the top and do not disturb the impurities at the bottom. If only part of the broth is to be used, push the fat aside before carefully removing the broth (do not mix any fat into the broth).

Note: To clarify broth, beat together 2 egg whites, pour them into the cold broth, and very gradually bring to a simmer. As the egg whites slowly cook, they will bring the impurities that cloud the broth to the surface. Use a skimmer to remove the egg whites and impurities.

ABOUT MINESTRE

Etruscan *puls* were thick combinations of grains, beans, and vegetables cooked together. They were the ancestors of Parma's *minestre,* which there are denser than minestrones. In Parma minestre can accurately be described as stew-soups, and are enjoyed as often as *zuppa* (soup) or minestrone. Most *minestre* are made without meat, with beans being the most frequent substitute—a good *minestra* can be a balanced one-pot meal.

MINESTRA DI RISO E CAVOLO

*RICE AND CABBAGE
MINESTRA*

SERVES 4

As this is more a stew than a soup, we customarily serve it as a main course. To make a meatless version, water is used in place of broth, but the minestra remains full of flavor. The use of red wine in this *minestra* is uniquely Parmesan. Some cooks add the wine immediately after the cooking, but I prefer to let each person add his or her own at the table.

> 1½ quarts meat broth (page 65) or good-quality store-bought
> 1 carrot
> 1 green celery rib
> 1 medium onion
> 2 teaspoons dried basil
> 1 teaspoon dried thyme
> 2 large bay leaves
> 4 cups 1-inch cubes cabbage
> 1 cup Italian or long-grain rice
> ½ cup peas (fresh or frozen)
> 1 scallion, thinly sliced
> Salt and pepper
> ¼ cup chopped parsley
> ½ cup red wine
> ½ cup freshly grated Parmigiano-Reggiano

Put the broth in a soup pot over medium heat. Dice the carrots, celery, and onion and add to the broth. When the broth reaches a slow boil, add the herbs. When the vegetables are about half-cooked, in about 20 minutes, add the cabbage and rice. When the rice is *al dente*, add the peas and scallion, season to taste with the salt and pepper, and continue to cook until the peas are cooked through but not mushy. Add the parsley and remove the pot from the heat. Pass the wine and the cheese at the table.

ABOUT BEANS

To prepare dried beans for cooking, soak the beans overnight in plenty of water. After soaking, they can be drained and cooked. For soup, cook them in the broth until *al dente*, then begin to add any other ingredients; the beans and other ingredients should finish cooking at the same time. Another method is to prepare the beans separately. After soaking, drain off the water and add I cup of fresh water or broth and I tablespoon of minced onion for each ½ cup of beans. Cover the beans and cook until tender, about 2 hours. Add additional water if necessary to keep the beans barely covered. The cooked beans can then be added to soup along with the other ingredients, as in the following recipe. If you cannot soak the beans overnight, bring a pot of water to a boil, add the beans, and return the water to a boil. Boil the beans for 2 minutes, cover them, and remove the pot from the heat. Let the beans stand for I hour, then proceed.

MINESTRA DI RISO E FAGIOLI

*T*his richly flavored and varied *minestra* is always served as a main course or a meal in itself.

¼ ounce dried mushrooms

2 quarts meat broth (page 65) or good-quality store-bought

2 medium carrots, trimmed and peeled

I large celery rib, trimmed and washed

I medium onion, wiped clean and stem removed

2 leek leaves, washed

I teaspoon dried basil

2 bay leaves

½ cup Italian or long-grain rice

4 ounces fresh peas

I zucchini, cut into ⅜-inch dice

I tomato, cut into ⅜-inch dice

½ cup dried cannellini beans

½ cup dried *toscanelli* beans

½ cup dried Roman beans

Salt and pepper

2 tablespoons chopped parsley

¼ cup freshly grated Parmigiano-Reggiano

Soak and cook the beans according to the method on page 68. Retain the cooking liquid.

Break up the mushrooms and soak in ¼ cup tepid broth to soften. Put the remaining broth in a soup pot and bring to a boil. Dice the carrots, celery, onion, and leeks, add them to the broth and add the basil and bay leaves. Bring the broth to a slow boil and add the softened mushrooms and their liquid. Cook the mixture for 20 minutes, add the rice, and simmer for 15 more minutes. Add the peas, zucchini, tomato, and beans with their liquid and continue to cook until everything is tender, about 15 more minutes. Season the *minestra* to taste with the salt and pepper, add the parsley, and serve with the cheese on the side.

OVERLEAF, CLOCKWISE
FROM TOP:
*Rice and Cabbage Minestra,
Anolini in Broth, Baked
Onion Soup, Minestra with
Lentils and Greens*

MINESTRA CON PISELLI E SPINACI

*PEA AND
SPINACH MINESTRA*

SERVES 4

A hearty pea soup that takes about 50 minutes to prepare. This highly
nutritious and substantial *minestra* is often a main course.

1½ quarts chicken broth (page 64) or good-quality store-bought
1½ pounds peas (fresh or frozen)
2 celery ribs
1 large carrot
1 medium onion, peeled
2 teaspoons dried basil
½ teaspoon dried thyme
1 bay leaf
1 pound fresh or 10 ounces frozen chopped spinach
4 tablespoons olive oil
1 large clove garlic, chopped
6 (¼-inch-thick) slices day-old Italian bread
1 tablespoon freshly grated Parmigiano-Reggiano

Put the broth and the peas into a soup pot over medium-high heat. Dice the
celery, carrots, and onion and add to the broth. Add the herbs and simmer
for 45 minutes, or until the vegetables are very soft. Pour the broth through
a strainer or sieve into another pot and use the back of a wooden spoon to
push the vegetables through—only the skins from the peas should remain in
the strainer. Add the spinach and simmer until cooked, about 5 minutes.

Preheat the oven to 425° F.

Heat the oil in a skillet and add the garlic. Brush garlic oil evenly on
both sides of the bread slices. Put *crostini* on a baking sheet and bake until
brown on top. Turn the *crostini* over, sprinkle with the cheese, and complete
the browning.

To serve, pour the *minestra* into bowls or large soup plates. Float half the
crostini on top and lean the rest against the sides of the bowls.

MINESTRA DI ORZO E FAGIOLI

*BARLEY AND
BEAN MINESTRA*

SERVES 4 TO 6

*M*ost people overlook barley when they think of Italian food. In fact, Italians have enjoyed barley and benefited from its nutritional value for centuries. This dish, another one-dish meal, is loaded with nutrients. After a day of business, my mother would cook this in her pressure cooker. My wife, Betty, puts everything in a slow cooker in the morning and when she gets home, dinner is ready, while I do it the old fashioned way. It is another *minestra* that is enhanced by the addition of red wine.

½ ounce dried mushrooms

⅓ cup dried Roman beans, soaked overnight (see box, page 68)

⅓ cup dried kidney beans, soaked overnight (see box, page 68)

⅓ cup dried *toscanelli* beans, soaked overnight (see box, page 68)

2 cups water

½ pound barley

¼ pound shin of prosciutto in 1 piece (available at Italian groceries
   or specialty foods shops)

2 cloves garlic, chopped

2 or 3 bay leaves

1 teaspoon dried thyme

2 to 2½ quarts meat broth (page 65) or good-quality store-bought

1 medium onion, peeled

1 carrot, trimmed and peeled

1 green celery rib, trimmed and washed

4 to 5 ounces peas (fresh or frozen)

½ cup diced fresh tomato

2 tablespoons chopped parsley

½ cup red wine

½ cup freshly grated Parmigiano-Reggiano

Break up the mushrooms and soak in tepid water to soften. Boil the beans in the 2 cups water for 10 minutes and strain. Rinse the barley under cool water. Put the beans, barley, prosciutto, garlic, thyme, and bay leaves in a soup pot and add 2 quarts broth. Simmer mixture, covered, for 1¼ hours, or until the beans and barley are tender, adding a little more broth if it all is absorbed. Add the mushrooms and their liquid to the pot. Dice the onion, carrot, and celery, add them to the pot, and simmer, covered, until the vegetables are tender. Add the peas and tomato and cook 10 to 15 more minutes. Sprinkle *minestra* with the parsley and remove the pot from the heat. Pass the wine and the cheese at the table.

MINESTRA DI LENTICCHIE CON ERBETTE

MINESTRA WITH LENTILS AND GREENS

SERVES 6

*M*ost of the time I cook up this hearty dish as a main course but it also can be served as a first course. Sometimes a piece of prosciutto shin is cooked with the lentils, but this version does not call for it. Without the broth—simply increase the water—this makes an excellent meatless meal.

2 cups dried lentils

2 quarts meat broth (page 65) or good-quality store-bought

1 teaspoon dried basil

1 clove garlic, chopped

1 medium onion, peeled

2 leek leaves or 2 scallions, trimmed

2 green celery ribs, trimmed and washed

2 carrots, trimmed and peeled

2 cups chopped Swiss chard or kale, leafy parts only

Salt and pepper

Put the lentils in a soup pot with 1½ quarts water, bring to boil, and strain. Put the broth in the pot and add the lentils and basil. Bring the mixture to a simmer and cover. Add the garlic to the pot. Dice the onion, leeks, celery, and carrots and add them to the broth when the lentils are soft. When the vegetables are half-cooked, add the greens and the salt and pepper to taste and cook until everything is tender, about 10 minutes.

Large *crostini* (page 76) are delicious with this *minestra*.

Minestra di Cotechino e Lenticchie

Aunt Lola's instructions to me for *cotechino* and lentils typifies the culinary concepts from the Val Taro kitchens of Parma. Her instructions are in both English and the dialect of the region:

"With a little oil *fi un bun sufri di cigula*—a good sauté with a variety of onions and a little thyme. If you wish, you can add herbs that you like with the lentils. No garlic, because there is garlic in the *cotechino.* Add the lentils and *brodo* to the *sufri.* It is best to precook the *cotechino* in plain water to get the fat out. Then transfer it to the lentils. You can cook the soup covered to keep in the flavors. If there is too much liquid at the end, cook it a little uncovered. Red wine in this is very good. I put a full glass in mine."

> I to I½ pounds *cotechino* (available at Italian groceries and
> specialty foods shops)
> 3 tablespoons olive oil
> ¼ cup chopped yellow onion
> I scallion, trimmed and thinly sliced
> ¼ cup chopped leeks
> I½ cups dried lentils
> I teaspoon dried thyme
> 3 bay leaves
> I cup red wine
> I½ to 2 quarts meat broth (page 65) or good-quality store-bought
> I cup chopped tomato (optional)
> ⅓ cup chopped fresh parsley

Put the *cotechino* in a soup pot with I½ quarts water, bring to a boil, and cook at a low boil for 45 minutes.

Meanwhile, in a soup pot heat the oil and sauté the onion, scallion, and leeks over medium heat until they are transluscent. Add the lentils, thyme, and bay leaves and mix well. Sauté mixture, stirring, for I or 2 minutes and add the wine, broth, and tomato. Bring mixture to a simmer and add the *cotechino* when it is ready. Cook the *minestra* until the lentils are soft, about I¾ hours. Mix in the parsley before serving.

ZUPPA DI CIPOLLE AL FORNO

This is one of the world's great soups. It is said that Catherine de Médici introduced this soup to France as queen to Henry II. Her Florentine cooks, who had moved with her, melted grated Parmigiano-Reggiano over the onions in the soup which was served at court. When I told my father the story, he replied, "and who taught the Florentines how to gratin Parma's great cheese?"

FOR THE ONION CROSTINI:

> 6 tablespoons butter
> 1 scallion, trimmed and thinly sliced
> ¼ medium onion, chopped
> ¼ cup chopped leeks
> ¼ cup chopped shallots (optional)
> 8 (½-inch-thick) slices day-old Italian bread

Preheat the oven to 400° F. Heat the butter in a skillet. Add the onions and sauté until limp and glazed but not browned.

Spread the onion mixture evenly on both sides of the bread slices. Put *crostini* on a baking sheet and bake until crispy on top. Turn the *crostini* over to complete browning. Remove the *crostini* and set aside.

FOR THE SOUP:

> 4 cups sliced onions
> 4 cups meat broth (page 65) or good-quality store-bought
> Salt and pepper
> ½ cup freshly grated Parmigiano-Reggiano

Preheat the oven to 450° F.

Put the onions and broth into a soup pot and bring to a slow boil. Cook until the onions are just limp and transluscent. Season to taste with salt and pepper. Transfer the soup to 1 big ovenproof crock or 4 individual soup crocks. Top the soup with *crostini* and sprinkle evenly with cheese. Put the crock(s) in the oven and bake the soup until the cheese melts and begins to brown, 15 to 20 minutes.

ANULIN IN BRODO

ANULIN IN BROTH

SERVES 6 TO 8

Without a doubt, *Anulin in Brodo* is our favorite soup. The Parmesan style of the Apennines is to combine similar flavors in the *anulin* filling and the broth. For example, here we have my mother's chicken-filled pasta bathed in its own broth for a weave of similar flavors.

> Salt
> ½ recipe *anulin* (page 44)
> 3 quarts chicken broth (page 64) or good-quality store-bought
> ½ cup freshly grated Parmigiano-Reggiano

Put about 5 quarts of water in a soup pot and bring to a boil. Add the salt and carefully drop in the *anulin*. Bring the broth to a simmer in another pot. As soon as the *anulin* rise to the surface—they are about half-cooked at this point—use a large skimmer or long-handled strainer to transfer them to the pot of broth and cook until *al dente*, about 8 minutes. If it is impractical to serve the soup immediately, the *anulin* may be held in warm broth for up to 20 minutes before cooking. When you are ready to serve, bring the broth to a simmer and cook the pasta until *al dente*.

Serve the soup from a warmed tureen and pass the cheese at the table.

ANOLINI IN BRODO

*I*n other areas of Parma, contrasting tastes in the *anolini* filling and the broth are preferred, as in this beef-filled pasta bathed in a broth made from chicken and veal as well as beef.

Salt
½ recipe *anolini* (page 42)
3 quarts meat broth (page 65) or good-quality store-bought
½ cup freshly grated Parmigiano-Reggiano

Put about 5 quarts of water in a soup pot and bring to a boil. Add the salt and carefully drop in the *anolini*. Bring the broth to a simmer in another pot. As soon as the *anolini* rise to the surface—they are about half-cooked at this point—use a large skimmer or long-handled strainer to transfer them to the pot of broth and cook until *al dente*, about 8 minutes. If it is impractical to serve the soup immediately, the *anolini* may be held in warm broth for up to 20 minutes before cooking. When you are ready to serve, bring the broth to a simmer and cook the pasta until *al dente*.

Serve the soup from a warmed tureen and pass the cheese at the table.

MEAT,
GAME,
POULTRY
AND FISH

For centuries, Parma has been known for its excellent methods of raising animals. Throughout the province there is first-rate beef, veal, lamb, horse, goat, and of course, pork. Here we will concentrate on typical meats and omit horse and goat, which are cooked only rarely in the United States and less frequently today in Parma. However, I have included some preparations for some less expensive cuts of meat that perhaps are not so familiar.

Veal

Veal is the most valued of Parma's fresh meats. Successful preparations depend on high-quality meat and expert handling, but all cuts are enjoyed—the shoulder, breast, and shin as much as any more expensive cut. Unless it is being cooked with a liquid, high-quality veal should never be cooked past medium-well. Regardless of the cooking technique though, the delicate taste of veal should always be the main objective.

PORK

For Parmigiani, the pig is not a sacred animal but is highly appreciated for its meat. When I was young, in early September, Nonno Guiseppe and his friends would have a festive day in Pine Plains, New York celebrating the season's bounty. Among Nonno's friends were Pio Bozzi and John Ganzi from the Palm steak house in New York City, Genu Costa, founder of the Surprise Rotisserie, a popular Harlem eatery for more than sixty years, and Yozzo, everyone's buddy.

In my memory, the day's event is captured as if on video. My father, his brother Frank, and Cousin Louie would slaughter the hogs while the rest of us "men" looked on. The three butchers would then section the animals and prepare the various cuts for curing. The yield would include prosciutto, coppa, sanguinaccio, pancetta, cotechino, and various kinds of salami.

Other activities were part of the day's celebration. First there was Yozzo and his winemaking crew; after giving them our seal of approval, we would proceed to the kitchen. Bozzi, Costa, Conti, Ganzi, and Sidoli put their cooking knowledge to work. Although I was a mature six-year-old, I cannot recall what we cooked. I took magnificent meals for granted and did not record that one.

GAME AND POULTRY

Among Parma's other meats are game birds, rabbit, and chicken which are turned into various preparations, but alla cacciatore is among the most popular. Poultry is plentiful throughout the province, provided precautions are made to protect the birds from the fox. Once the post-Columbian food exchange got underway and the turkey made its way to Europe, it became popular in Parma, and in time replaced the peacock as a favorite for festive meals.

FISH

Italy is a peninsula with a distinguished reputation for seafood. The land-locked provinces like Parma, however, are dependent on lakes and rivers for fish. There are small lakes in Parma, and the Po, Parma, Ceno, and Taro rivers all run through the province. Anglers are a familar sight, particularly along the Taro. A variety of freshwater fish are seduced by their lures, but the catch prized above all is the trout.

STRACOTTO DI MANZO DI PARMA

PARMA'S POT ROAST

SERVES 4

*T*he tomatoes in this recipe are an excellent example of the Parmigiano variation on an ancient preparation using a food from the New World.

¼ cup olive oil

4 tablespoons butter

I (4-pound) top round of beef

⅓ cup flour

I medium onion

I celery rib, trimmed and washed

I large carrot, trimmed and peeled

3 to 4 cloves garlic

2 bay leaves

I tablespoon dried sage

I½ cups dry red wine

2 cups meat broth (page 65) or good-quality store-bought

½ cup chopped tomato

I recipe potato *gnocchi* (page 56)

¼ cup chopped fresh parsley

Salt and pepper

¼ cup freshly grated Parmigiano-Reggiano

Preheat the oven to 425° F. Put the oil and butter in a deep roasting pan. Dredge the beef in the flour, put it into the pan, and place in the oven. Dice the onion, celery, carrot, and garlic and add. Roast the beef, turn after 10 minutes until browned on all sides. Add the herbs and cook for 1 minute.

Add the wine and lower the oven temperature to 350° F. Cook the meat for 10 minutes, add the broth and tomato, and cover. After 45 minutes, turn the meat. After another 45 minutes check for tenderness; if tender, add the parsley and salt and pepper and cook, uncovered, for 10 minutes, turn and cook 5 minutes. Remove the meat from the pan and allow the juices to cool a bit. Remove any fat from the surface of the juices. Loosen the browned bits from the bottom of the pan with a spatula, and purée the defatted juices and vegetables, using a food mill or processor.

Slice the beef and arrange on a platter with the *gnocchi*. Ladle on some sauce, sprinkle with 1 tablespoon cheese. Pass the remaining sauce and cheese.

BRASATO DI MANZO DELLA VAL TARO

POT ROAST FROM THE VAL TARO

SERVES 4 TO 6

*B*ecause this pot roast has more ingredients than Parma's potted beef, and it must be turned more frequently, I take the easy way out and cook it on top of the stove, so I don't have to open and close the oven so often.

Typically in Parma, many dishes are prepared with more than one meal in mind. This is a good example; the leftover beef is used in pasta fillings, and the juices as sauces for pasta or polenta.

3 tablespoons olive oil
I (4-pound) bottom round of beef
¼ cup flour
I medium onion, chopped
½ teaspoon dried sage
½ teaspoon dried rosemary
I teaspoon dried basil
2 or 3 bay leaves
I cup dry red wine
2 cups meat broth (page 65) or good-quality store-bought
2 carrots
2 green celery ribs
¼ pound white turnips (optional)
6 small white onions
¼ cup chopped fresh parsley
I cup fresh or frozen peas (optional)
Salt and pepper
I recipe potato *gnocchi* (page 56)
⅓ cup freshly grated Parmigiano-Reggiano

Heat the oil in a deep heavy pot. Dredge the beef in the flour, carefully put it in the hot oil, and brown it on all sides. Add the onion to brown with the meat and mix in the herbs. Add the wine, cover the pot tightly, and boil for 3 minutes. Add the broth, cover the pot tightly, and lower the heat to maintain at a simmer.

Clean and cut the carrots, celery, and turnips into ½-inch pieces and clean and peel the onions. After the pot roast has cooked for 1½ hours and is almost tender, add the vegetables. Cover the pot tightly and continue to

simmer for 1 more hour, or until the meat and vegetables are tender. Add the parsley, peas, and salt and pepper to taste near the end of cooking and cook, uncovered, for 15 minutes.

To serve, cut pot roast into ¼-inch slices and arrange in a serving dish. Surround the pot roast with the vegetables and top with the sauce. Serve the *gnocchi* on a separate plate topped with some sauce and cheese.

The excess meat can be used to make a filling for ravioli (page 50) or *anolini* (page 42), and any remaining sauce may be used for pasta.

A PRIZED ROAST

For a succulent, tender, firm roast accompanied by its natural juices, in a roasting pan with ¼ inch of liquid begin the roasting in a very hot oven to sear the outer surface of the roast, then lower the temperature to cook slowly. Searing the meat helps to seal in the juices, and lowering the temperature allows the meat to cook more evenly and minimizes shrinkage. Immediately after roasting, strain the pan juices into a bowl and put them in the freezer. Let the roast rest, loosely covered with punctured aluminum foil. (The old-timers would throw a clean white cloth over the roast to prevent a chill.) When the roast is ready to be carved, remove the pan juices from the freezer and skim the fat from the surface. Pour the defatted juices into a saucepan, add any juices that may have escaped from the roast, and bring to a simmer for 15 to 30 seconds. The roast may be served sliced, with the juices ladled over the meat, or the juices may be served on the side.

ARROSTO DI MANZO

Roast Beef

SERVES 6 TO 8

What a surprise and delight it was for me to discover rare roast beef in Parma. This is a popular dish, and different cuts of beef are used depending on one's preference.

6 pounds boneless rib eye, sirloin roast, top round, or eye round
Salt and pepper
1 to 1½ cups meat broth (page 65) or good-quality store-bought (optional)
Preheat the oven to 450° F.

Remove most of the fat from the rib eye and sprinkle with the salt and pepper to taste. Put the rib eye on the rack of a roasting pan, pour ½ inch broth or water into the pan, and roast meat for 30 minutes. Lower the temperature to 325° F., and roast meat for 1 hour. The roast should be cooked rare. To test for doneness, plunge a kitchen fork into the center of the meat. It should come out just warm to the lip or inside of the wrist.

BISTECCA FRITTA AL VIN ROSSO CON RISOTTO

BEEF STEAK SAUTÉED IN RED WINE WITH RISOTTO

SERVES 2

1 (10-ounce) chuck steak, cut into 2 (5-ounce) steaks
⅛ to ¼ cup flour
3 tablespoons butter
½ cup dry red wine
1 bay leaf
1 to 1½ cups meat broth (page 65) or good-quality store-bought
1 recipe *risotto vin rosso* (page 32)

Dredge the steaks in the flour. Heat the butter in a medium sauté pan over medium-high heat, and brown the steaks thoroughly on both sides. Add the wine and bay leaf and cook to reduce the wine by half. Add the broth and bring it to a low boil. Cook the steaks, covered, for about 10 minutes, turn them, and cook, covered, 10 more minutes. Fork-test for doneness. If the steaks are tender, uncover them and cook until the liquid is reduced to about ¼ cup, turning the steaks about halfway through the reduction.

Serve the steaks with the *risotto vin rosso*.

OSSO BUCO CON RISOTTO ALLO ZAFFERANO

VEAL SHANKS WITH SAFFRON RISOTTO

SERVES 6

Nonno Giuseppe taught his son Camillo, my father, the way he cooked *osso buco* for Enrico Caruso. It was Nonno's recipe that we used at Camillo Restaurant, and we always sold out of this classic veal shank preparation. The shanks may be cooked whole or they may be cut in half—my preference is for tied whole shanks. The smaller cut *ossi buchi* cook faster and are served two to a person. Depending on my mood, I prepare this dish on top of the stove or in the oven. Below is the oven method. *Osso buco* may be made up to two days in advance or early on the day it is to be served and reheated; it often benefits from being made ahead. The accompanying risotto should be a little *asciutto*—dryish—because the *osso buco* sauce is poured over it.

½ ounce dried *porcini* mushrooms

1 cup dry white wine

¼ cup olive oil

4 tablespoons butter

6 veal shanks (whole tied or halved)

½ cup flour

1 onion, peeled

1 carrot, peeled

1 celery rib, trimmed and washed

1 teaspoon chopped garlic

½ teaspoon dried basil

½ teaspoon dried thyme

2 bay leaves

1 to 1½ cups meat broth (page 65) or good-quality store-bought

½ cup chopped tomato (optional)

1 tablespoon chopped fresh parsley

Salt and pepper

1 recipe *risotto allo zafferano* (page 35)

Preheat the oven to 425° F.

Soak the mushrooms in the wine to soften.

Heat the oil and the butter in a casserole. Dredge the veal shanks in the flour, add them to the casserole, and brown them in the oven. As the veal is browning, dice the onion, carrot, and celery and add them to the casserole. Drain the softened mushrooms, squeezing to extract as much of the liquid as possible, and reserve the soaking liquid. Chop the mushrooms and add them to the casserole. When the veal is browned, add the garlic and as it begins to brown, stir in the herbs. Add the reserved soaking liquid and cook the veal, covered, for 5 minutes. Add the broth, lower the oven temperature to 350° F., and cook, covered, for 2 more hours, turning the *osso buco* occasionally. Uncover the casserole and add the tomato, parsley, and salt and pepper to taste. (This is a good time to begin the risotto.) When the tomato is cooked, all the flavors should be blended and the veal should be tender and falling off the bone.

To serve, arrange the *osso buco* in the middle of a platter and surround it with the risotto. Pour a little sauce over both *osso buco* and risotto and pass the remaining sauce at the table.

PETTO DI VITELLO RIPIENO DI CAMILLO

▰▰▰▰▰▰▰▰▰

CAMILLO'S STUFFED
BREAST OF VEAL

SERVES 10 TO 12

*T*his was my father's favorite. He enjoyed this dish both in Parma and at home in New York. It is a true classic that rates with the best.

4 pounds fresh spinach or 4 (10-ounce) packages chopped frozen spinach

½ ounce dried *porcini* mushrooms

1 cup milk

1½ to 2 cups cubed 2-day-old bread

4 tablespoons butter

1 medium onion, finely chopped

3 scallions, trimmed and finely sliced

5 ounces very fresh *mascarpone* or other soft cheese at room temperature

¾ cup freshly grated Parmigiano-Reggiano

¼ teaspoon freshly grated nutmeg

3 eggs

2 teaspoons chopped fresh rosemary

2 teaspoons chopped fresh sage

2 teaspoons chopped fresh tarragon

1 (6-pound breast) of veal with pocket (see note below)

2 cups meat broth (page 65) or good-quality store-bought

Salt and pepper

If using fresh spinach, trim the stems and wash the leaves thoroughly. Cook the fresh spinach in lightly salted boiling water, refresh it immediately under cold water, and squeeze it as dry as possible. Chop the spinach and reserve.

Soak the *porcini* in half the milk to soften. Soak the bread in the remaining milk.

Heat the butter in a sauté pan and stir in the onion and scallions. Strain the *porcini* over the soaking bread and squeeze the excess milk from the *porcini* onto the bread. Chop the porcini and add them to the pan. Sauté the mixture until all the vegetables are limp.

Add the sautéed vegetables, spinach, cheeses, nutmeg, and eggs to the bread and mix together thoroughly. Fill the veal pocket with the stuffing.

Preheat the oven to 425° F.

Combine the herbs. Put the veal on a rack in a roasting pan and sprinkle it with the salt and pepper and the herb mixture. Pour the broth into the pan and roast the veal for 20 minutes. Lower the oven temperature to 325° F. and roast the veal for 2½ to 3 hours, or until a fork plunged into the center of the stuffing comes out hot. The veal should be cooked medium-well. Remove the veal from the pan and let it rest for 30 minutes before carving. Pour the pan juices into a container and put it in the freezer. Just before serving, remove the fat from the surface of the juices and warm them.

To serve, carve 2 slices per bone, as with prime rib. Serve the juices on the side.

Note: Have the butcher prepare a pocket for stuffing and crack the joints for easy carving after roasting, or have the pocket made and the breast boned. Keep the bones and set the veal on them while roasting. I like to leave the bone in.

VITELLO ARROSTO CON VERDURE MISTE

Roast Veal with Mixed Vegetables

SERVES 6

1 (3- to 3½-pound) veal roast (boned and tied shoulder of veal
    or boneless round of veal, tied)

1 pound small white onions

1 celery rib

1 pound baby carrots

1 teaspoon dried thyme

1 or 2 bay leaves

1 cup dry white wine

2 cups meat broth (page 65) or good-quality store-bought

Salt and pepper

4 tablespoons butter

1 cup fresh or frozen peas (optional)

Preheat the oven to 425° F.

Rinse the veal under cool water, dry well, and put in a flameproof roasting pan. Brown the meat on all sides in the oven. Clean the onions, celery, and carrots and chop the celery into 1-inch pieces and add the vegetables to the pan. Lower the oven temperature to 350° F. and roast veal for 10 minutes. Mix in the herbs, add the wine, and cook 5 more minutes. Add the broth and roast the veal, covered, until it is well done and tender, about 2 hours.

Remove the veal from the pan and let it rest for 30 minutes. Pour the pan juices into a bowl and place them in the freezer. Melt the butter in the pan with the vegetables and add the peas and salt and pepper to taste. Remove the fat from the reserved pan juices. Put the pan on top of the stove and brown the vegetables over medium heat. Return the veal to the pan, add ¾ cup of the reserved juices, and heat thoroughly. Arrange the veal on a platter and surround it with the vegetables.

Umido di Vitello Robusto con Polenta

Robust Veal Casserole with Polenta

SERVES 6

With this veal casserole we generally serve polenta, but *risotto robusto* or potatoes cooked with the veal are other excellent choices. I generally cook this dish in the oven as a casserole, but it also can be cooked on top of the stove and finished in the oven.

2 tablespoons olive oil

1½ pounds stewing veal, cut into 1½-inch cubes from the shoulder, breast, or rib end of the neck, boned with fat and sinew removed

About ¼ cup flour

1 medium onion

1 clove garlic

1 cup pearl onions, cleaned and peeled

1 tablespoon dried basil

¼ teaspoon dried oregano

¼ teaspoon dried thyme

1 cup chopped or crushed canned tomatoes

1½ cups meat broth (page 65) or good-quality store-bought

Salt and pepper

1 recipe polenta (page 29)

Preheat the oven to 450° F.

Put the oil in a casserole and heat it in oven. Dredge the veal in the flour and carefully add it to the hot oil.

Chop the white onion and garlic. When the veal begins to brown, add the white onion, garlic, pearl onions, and herbs, cook for 1 to 2 minutes, and stir in the tomatoes, broth, and salt and pepper to taste. Lower the oven temperature to 350° F. and cook the veal for about 10 minutes. Cover the casserole and cook the veal for about 30 minutes. Uncover casserole and cook until the veal and vegetables are tender, about 20 more minutes. Serve the veal and vegetables with the polenta.

UMIDO DI VITELLO DELICATO CON GNOCCHI

DELICATE VEAL CASSEROLE

SERVES 6

4 tablespoons vegetable oil

1½ pounds stewing veal, cut into 1½-inch cubes from the shoulder, breast, or rib end of the neck, boned with fat and sinew removed

About ¼ cup flour

1½ teaspoons dried marjoram or basil

½ cup dry white wine

1 cup meat broth (page 65) or good-quality store-bought

1 cup small pearl onions, cleaned and peeled

½ pound baby carrots

Salt and pepper

½ recipe potato *gnocchi* (page 56)

Preheat the oven to 425° F.

Put the oil in a casserole and heat it in the oven. Dredge the veal in the flour, carefully add it to the hot oil, and brown the veal in the oven. Add the marjoram and wine, lower the oven temperature to 350° F., and cook the veal, covered, for 5 minutes. Stir in the broth and simmer, with the cover slightly ajar, until the veal is almost tender, about 1 hour.

Add the onions, carrots, and salt and pepper to taste to the veal and cook until the vegetables are tender, about 25 minutes. When the veal is ready, cook the *gnocchi* in boiling salted water, drain them, and add to the veal. Serve at once.

INVOLTINI DI VITELLO

*Stuffed Veal
Envelopes*

Serves 4

*A*nother specialty from Camillo. For the stuffing we use Parma's famous
ham and famous cheese.

8 (3-ounce) veal escalopes

8 slices proscuitto

8 large fresh sage leaves

½ cup freshly grated Parmigiano-Reggiano

½ cup chopped fresh parsley

Fresh black pepper

4 tablespoons butter

½ cup flour

10 ounces sliced fresh *porcini*, *cremini*, or Porto bella mushrooms, trimmed
and wiped or rinsed if necessary

½ cup dry white wine

1 cup meat broth (page 65) or good-quality store-bought

Salt and pepper

Lay the veal escalopes flat on a butcher block or table. Put a slice of
proscuitto on each escalope, and arrange a sage leaf in the middle of each
proscuitto slice. Put a heaping teaspoon of cheese on each sage leaf and
sprinkle each with about ⅛ teaspoon of parsley and pepper to taste. Fold
each escalope in half over the cheese. To make the *involtini* leak-proof, fold in
the edges of each envelope and skewer a large wooden toothpick just under
the filling and from edge to edge.

Melt the butter in a sauté pan and dredge the veal in the flour. When
the butter begins to foam, carefully add the veal and mushrooms. Brown the
veal on both sides and add the wine. Bring the wine to a simmer and cook
for 30 seconds. Turn the veal and simmer for 30 more seconds. Add the
broth and return to a simmer. Reduce the cooking liquid by one third and
turn the veal again. Reduce liquid again by one third. When the veal is fork-
tender, in about 20 minutes, add 2 tablespoons parsley and salt and pepper
to taste. Serve *involtini* covered with sauce and mushrooms.

FETTE DI VITELLO ALLA GRIGLIA

Grilled Veal
Steaks
SERVES 2

*T*his has been a favorite of my wife, Betty, ever since I courted her at Camillo Restaurant. She met me late one evening, anticipating a night out on the town and the truth is it was actually my father and his staff who courted her. What Betty loves about this grilled veal is its tender, delicate flavor. The veal looks pretty on a plate next to a generous sprig of Italian parsley, a tangle of watercress, and a lemon wedge, and is especially good with grilled vegetables.

> ¼ cup olive oil
> Juice of ½ a lemon
> Salt and pepper
> 2 (7- to 8-ounce) veal steaks (see note below)

Prepare a charcoal fire or preheat the broiler.

Put the oil, lemon juice, and salt and pepper to taste in a shallow dish and marinate the veal 5 to 10 minutes on each side.

Cook the veal 3 to 7 minutes on each side, depending on the cooking method used and desired degree of doneness. The veal should be cooked rare to medium-well but never well done.

Note: Veal steaks are best cut from the top round of veal. Have the butcher cut them about ¾ inch thick. Supermarket veal shoulder steaks also work well in this dish.

UCCELLI DI VITELLO

VEAL "BIRDS"

SERVES 4

A day or so after a meal of filled pasta, we always looked forward to devouring *rolattini*, or veal "birds," a delicate dish that utilizes the excess filling for pasta such as *tortelli* or ravioli.

8 (2½- to 3-ounce) veal escalopes
½ to ¾ cup pasta filling (page 46 or 50)
6 ounces Fontina or Münster, cut into 8 wedges about the size of your index finger
⅓ cup flour
4 to 6 tablespoons butter
½ cup dry white wine
Juice of ½ a lemon
1 cup meat broth (page 65) or good-quality store-bought
Salt and pepper

Lay the veal escalopes on a butcher block or table. Put a tablespoon of filling on each escalope and top with cheese. Roll the veal over the filling and the cheese and secure with a large wooden toothpick. Dredge the veal in the flour, brushing off the excess.

Heat the butter in a sauté pan. When the butter begins to foam, add the *rolattini* and brown on all sides. Add the wine, lemon juice, and salt and pepper to taste and simmer the veal for 3 to 4 minutes. Add the broth and simmer, turning once or twice, for 15 to 20 more minutes, or until the veal is tender.

ARISTA DI MAIALE ARROSTO

Roast Loin of Pork

Serves 6 to 8

Once the prosciutto is prepared for curing, other cuts are prepared fresh. A juicy well-cooked roast pork loin is highly desirable for a fall dinner and, indeed, throughout most of the year. I prefer to cook the loin with its bone in because it cooks up juicier and more flavorful than a boneless loin. Most supermarket pork loins and chops are very lean, and will easily dry out if overcooked. Add water to the pan, if necessary, to prevent the pork from drying out in the later stages of roasting.

> I (6-pound) pork loin, bone in (see note below)
> ½ teaspoon dried sage
> ½ teaspoon dried thyme
> ½ scallion, trimmed and thinly sliced
> Salt and pepper

Preheat the oven to 450° F.

Put the pork loin on a rack in a roasting pan and fill pan with ¼ inch water. Rub the meat with the sage, thyme, and scallion and sprinkle with the salt and pepper to taste. Roast the pork loin in the oven for 30 to 40 minutes. Add more water if necessary. Lower the oven temperature to 325° F. and roast for 2 to 2½ more hours. A fork plunged into the center of the roast near the bone should come out hot but the meat should be juicy. Strain the pan juices into a bowl and put them in the freezer. Let the pork loin rest for about 30 minutes before serving. Remove the fat from the pan juices and serve them on the side.

Note: Have the butcher crack the back bone for easy carving after roasting.

COTECHINO CON POLENTA

Cotechino
with Polenta

SERVES 4

*C*otechino is a favorite sausage for most of us Parmigiani. Each hamlet or household will vary the serving of this dish. The polenta may be served plain with Parmigiano-Reggiano sprinkled on it and the *cotechino* served on the side, or the polenta may be covered with tomato sauce and slices of *cotechino*—with numerous versions in between. This is how we serve it. It also is good with left-over polenta cut into squares and pan-fried with sautéed cabbage on the side.

Cotechino should first be boiled in plain water, which draws out excess fat and salt. At least one change of water is necessary, but I generally change 3 times.

> A 1½-pound *cotechino*
> 1 recipe medium-ground polenta (page 29)
> 1 recipe *salsa di pomodoro e funghi* (page 59)
> ¼ pound Fontina or Münster
> ½ cup freshly grated Parmigiano-Reggiano

Bring a large pot of water to a boil. With a fork prick the *cotechino* all over. When the water begins to boil, add the *cotechino* and cook at a medium boil. After 20 minutes, bring a second pot of water to a boil. When the second pot begins to boil, transfer the *cotechino* from the first pot to the second. Repeat until the water is clear of fat.

While the *cotechino* is cooking, prepare the polenta and tomato sauce. When everything is ready, pour half the hot polenta onto a serving plate and cover it with the Fontina and half the Parmigiano-Reggiano. Pour the remaining polenta over the cheese and cover it with the sauce. Sprinkle the remaining Parmigiano-Reggiano on top. Peel the casing off the *cotechino*, slice it, and arrange it around the polenta.

POLENTA FRITTA CON COTECHINO E UOVA

FRIED POLENTA WITH COTECHINO AND EGGS

SERVES 4

*T*his is a quick meal using previously cooked polenta and *cotechino*. Occasionally we substitute *luganega* sausage. This was Nonno Giuseppe's favorite breakfast and makes a fabulous brunch dish.

¼ cup olive oil plus additional if necessary
½ recipe polenta (page 29), cooked and cooled a day in advance
½ of a cooked *cotechino*
8 eggs

Heat the oil in a large sauté pan. Cut the polenta into 8 (2- by 3-inch) pieces and carefully add them to the hot oil. Brown the polenta on 1 side and turn it, adding additional oil if necessary. Cut the *cotechino* into 8 pieces and add them to the pan. Turn the *cotechino* when browned. Crack the eggs and stir them into the pan. When the eggs are cooked to your liking, remove them and serve.

Cosciotto di Agnello Arrostito con Erbe Aromatiche

Herbed Roast Leg of Lamb

SERVES 10

*F*ragrant with many herbs, this special Easter Sunday dish is also enjoyed on other occasions.

I leg of lamb (about 6 pounds), whole or boned and tied
3 cloves garlic
I teaspoon dried oregano
I teaspoon dried sage
I tablespoon dried rosemary
I tablespoon dried marjoram
I tablespoon dried basil
I teaspoon dried thyme
2 cups meat broth (page 65) or good-quality store-bought
Salt and pepper
10 small white onions, cleaned

Preheat the oven to 450° F.

With a sharp paring knife make three I-inch slits in the lamb and place a garlic clove into each slit.

In a bowl combine the herbs and spread over the lamb. Pour broth into a roasting pan, put lamb on a rack in the pan, and add the onions. Roast the lamb in the oven for 30 minutes. Lower the temprature to 325° F. and continue to roast lamb for 2 to 2½ hours, or for 18 to 30 minutes per pound total cooking time, depending on desired doneness. Remove the lamb from the pan and let it rest, loosely covered with punctured aluminum foil, for about 15 to 30 minutes before carving. Pour the pan juices into a container and put it in the freezer. Just before serving, remove the fat from the surface of the pan juices and warm them. Slice the lamb and serve it with some of the juices and the onions; serve the remaining juices on the side.

Agnello in Umido con Polenta

*Lamb Casserole
with Polenta*

A robust, inexpensive dish that requires a little attention. This preparation also can be used for lamb shanks, but they will take longer to cook; *capretto*—baby goat—is good in this dish as well. I cook this casserole in the oven, but it also can be cooked on top of the stove.

2 tablespoons olive oil

1½ pounds stewing lamb, cut into 1½-inch cubes from the shoulder, neck, or leg, with fat and sinew removed

3 tablespoons flour

I medium onion, peeled

I scallion, trimmed

2 cloves garlic, peeled

2 teaspoons dried basil

I teaspoon dried thyme

I teaspoon dried oregano

2 bay leaves

I cup meat broth (page 65) or good-quality store-bought

5 medium carrots, trimmed and peeled

I (28-ounce) can whole tomatoes

I cup new peas, fresh or frozen

Salt and pepper

I recipe polenta (page 29)

Preheat the oven to 450° F.

Spread the oil in a roasting pan or ovenproof casserole. Put the lamb in the pan, sprinkle it with the flour, and put it in the oven. Chop the onion, scallion, and garlic and mix them in with the lamb. Roast the lamb, turning it from time to time, until it is browned all over, blend in the herbs, and add the broth Lower the oven temprature to 350° F., break up the tomatoes, and add them with their liquid to the pan. Cover the pan and cook for 30 minutes. Cut the carrots into half-inch cylinders, add them to the pan, and cook, covered, for 30 minutes, until the meat is tender. Remove the lid and cook lamb for 10 more minutes, or until the pan juices begin to thicken a little. (This is a good time to begin the polenta.) Add the peas and salt and pepper to taste and cook, uncovered, for about 8 minutes.

ABOUT CACCIATORA

There are basic methods of food preparation common to Italian cuisine in general, but they usually vary from region to region. One such basic preparation is *alla cacciatora*, or "hunter's style," by which small game, usually fowl, would provide the hunter's family with a savory meal.

In Parma, *cacciatora* is centuries old, and we believe it predates the introduction of the tomato in Italian cuisine. Our *cacciatora* requires three basic ingredients that refine and tame the wild flavors in game: onion, mushroom, and a cooking liquid. The sweetness and pungency of the onion tame the gaminess, the complex flavors of the mushroom complement the meat, and the cooking liquid softens and infuses the meat with the desired texture, strength, and blend of flavors.

My earliest recollection of *cacciatora* was during my annual fall visits to Nonno Giuseppe's resort in Pine Plains, New York. There, the hunters would bring in small game while my grandmother would take me foraging for wild mushrooms. If fresh mushrooms were not in sufficient abundance, she would use dried mushrooms in the *cacciatora*. That was the way of the mountains of Val Taro.

FAGIANO MARIA LUISA CON POLENTA

PHEASANT MARIA LOUISE WITH POLENTA

SERVES 4 TO 6

*I*f you brought Zia Maria a pheasant or other game bird, she would prepare this succulent *cacciatora* and always remind us that her ancestors cooked wild birds in this fashion for Maria Luisa, the duchess of Parma.

I (4- to 4½-pound) pheasant or other game bird such as quail, grouse, partridge, or woodcock, dressed

½ cup flour

⅓ cup olive oil or about 5 tablespoons butter

I large onion, peeled

¾ pound fresh *porcini* or *cremini* mushrooms, trimmed and wiped or rinsed as necessary

2 ounces dry vermouth

1½ cup dry white wine

2 or more cups meat broth (page 65) or good-quality store-bought

2 recipes medium-ground polenta (page 29)

Salt and pepper

½ cup chopped fresh parsley

I chopped scallion

½ cup freshly grated Parmigiano-Reggiano

Cut the game bird into 10 pieces (if using quail, leave them whole or cut in half), rinse the pieces and pat them dry and dredge in the flour. Heat the oil in a large sauté pan over medium heat and carefully add the bird, skin side down. Cook the bird, turning the pieces, until golden brown on all sides.

Slice the onion and mushrooms and add them to the pan. Lower the heat if necessary to avoid burning the vegetables.

When the bird is browned, add the vermouth, bring to a simmer, and add the wine. Boil the mixture over medium heat for 5 minutes, or until the cooking liquid is reduced by half. Add enough broth to cover the meat, bring to a simmer, and cover the pan. (This is a good time to start the polenta.)

Simmer the bird, covered, occasionally turning the pieces, until tender, about 1 hour. (Smaller birds may take less time, and some birds may take a little longer.) When the bird is tender, remove the lid and cook the sauce to reduce by half. Add the parsley and scallion and simmer for 2 minutes.

To serve, pour the polenta onto a platter and surround it with the *cacciatora*. Ladle the sauce over all and sprinkle one third of the cheese over the polenta. Serve the *cacciatora* at once and pass the remaining cheese at the table.

Coniglio alla Cacciatora con Polenta

Rabbit "Hunter's Style" with Polenta

Serves 4 to 6

1 (3- to 4-pound) rabbit, dressed

About ½ cup flour

⅓ cup olive oil

1 medium onion

¾ pound fresh *porcini* or *cremini* mushrooms, trimmed and wiped or rinsed clean as necessary

1½ teaspoons dried sage

2 bay leaves

⅔ cup dry red wine

1½ cups meat broth (page 65) or good-quality store-bought

Salt and pepper

1 recipe polenta (page 29)

½ cup freshly grated Parmigiano-Reggiano

Rinse the rabbit under cold water, pat it dry, cut it into 8 pieces, and dredge it in the flour. Heat the oil in a large sauté pan over medium heat and add the rabbit. Slice the onion lengthwise and add it to the pan. Slice the mushrooms and add them to the pan. Cook the rabbit, turning the pieces, until golden brown on all sides. Stir in the sage and bay leaves, add the wine, and bring to a slow boil. Cook 5 minutes, or until the wine is reduced by half. Add the broth and simmer, covered, until the rabbit is tender, about 40 to 50 minutes. (This is a good time the start the polenta.) Remove the lid, raise the heat, and reduce the cooking liquid by half, adding the salt and pepper to taste.

To serve, pour the polenta onto a platter and surround it with the *cacciatora*. Ladle the sauce over all and sprinkle one third of the cheese over the polenta. Serve the *cacciatora* at once and pass the remaining cheese at the table.

POLLO ALLA CACCIATORA CON POLENTA

CHICKEN "HUNTER'S STYLE" WITH POLENTA

SERVES 4

The outdoorsman adapted his barnyard bird for this dish when small game was unavailable, and he altered the ingredients to blend with the domesticated fowl. After the tomato was introduced to Italy, a little bit was added to this ancient northern Apennine dish. However, more than a little tomato drastically changes the flavor, and the dish can no longer be considered *cacciatora*. If you don't have a good fresh tomato in season, leave it out of this preparation.

2 recipes polenta (page 29)
I (3-pound) chicken
½ cup flour
½ cup butter
I medium onion, diced
2 cups sliced fresh *porcini* or *cremini* mushrooms
½ teaspoon dried basil
½ teaspoon dried marjoram
½ cup dry white wine
½ to I cup chicken broth (page 64) or good-quality store-bought
½ medium tomato, diced (optional)
I to 2 tablespoons chopped fresh parsley
Salt and pepper

Cut the chicken into 10 pieces, rinse and pat it dry, and dredge it in the flour. Heat the butter in a large sauté pan over medium heat and carefully add the chicken, skin side down. Cook the chicken, turning when the skin side is brown, and add the onion and mushrooms. When the chicken is browned on all sides, add the herbs and cook about one minute. Add the wine and bring it to a boil. (This is a good time to start the polenta.) Add the broth and return the mixture to a boil. Lower the heat and simmer 20 minutes, or until the chicken is tender. Add the tomato, parsley, and salt and pepper to taste and simmer 10 more minutes.

To serve, pour the polenta onto a platter and surround it with the *cacciatora*. Ladle the sauce over all.

PEZZI DI POLLO CON PATATE E FUNGHI AL FORNO

CHICKEN BAKED WITH POTATOES AND MUSHROOMS

SERVES 4

This is a great dish for a busy schedule. Just pop it in a hot oven and come back in about 45 minutes. No fat is added to this dish: The drippings from the chicken will prevent sticking. The natural flavors of the chicken, mushrooms, and potatoes intermingle and provide a delicate combination of tastes, so no herbs are needed.

4 potatoes
I (3-pound) chicken
10 ounces fresh *cremini* mushrooms, wiped clean and left whole
Salt and pepper

Preheat the oven to 400° F.

Clean and cut the potatoes lengthwise into wedges, about ½ inch thick. In a sauté pan bring ½ inch of salted water to a boil. Add the potatoes, and cover the pot. Cook the potatoes half-way, for about 8 minutes, and drain them. Cut the chicken into quarters or smaller pieces, rinse it under cold water, and dry it well. Wipe the mushrooms clean; leave them whole. Put the chicken, potatoes, and mushrooms in a roasting pan, sprinkle with the salt and pepper, and bake for 45 minutes.

OVERLEAF: *Bollito Misto and its traditional accompaniments, Mostarda di Frutta, Salsa Verde, Vinaigrette*

BOLLITO MISTO

Mixed Boiled Meats

SERVES 8

*B*ollito misto is Parma's boiled dinner. The final touch here has a subtle "modern" twist—half-green tomato and roasted sweet peppers from the Americas in the vinaigrette—so it isn't quite the same dish the Longobards craved when they arrived in Parma. This is a large, satisfying dish that needs only the addition of a green salad, and, while hearty, is suitable for celebrations like New Year's Day. A fruit tart makes a nice ending.

I (2-pound) *cotechino*
I pound beef brisket
I pound veal tongue
2 bay leaves
¼ teaspoon whole peppercorns
2 cloves garlic
I pound veal brisket
I (2½-pound) chicken
I½ gallons water
6 carrots, peeled
6 celery ribs, trimmed and washed
6 medium onions, peeled
I recipe *salsa verde* (recipe follows)
I recipe vinaigrette (page 21)
I (12-ounce) jar *mostarda di frutta* (see note below)

Prepare the *cotechino* according to the method given in the recipe for *Cotechino con Polenta* (page 99).

While the *cotechino* is cooking in a large pot bring the water to a boil and add the beef brisket, veal tongue, bay leaves, peppercorns, and garlic. Lower the heat and simmer, covered, for I½ hours. Add the veal brisket and simmer, covered, I hour. Add the chicken and simmer, covered, for 30 minutes. Add the carrots, celery, and onions and simmer, covered, until everything is cooked, about 30 more minutes. The misto may be kept in the broth for 30 to 45 minutes before serving. Keep the broth for another use.

Remove the meats from the broth with a kitchen fork, holding them over the pot to drain off excess broth, and arrange on a serving platter or cutting board. Slice the meats using a carving knife and a kitchen fork. Surround the meats with the vegetables. Serve *bollito misto* with *salsa verde*, vinaigrette, and *mostarda di frutta*.

Note: *Mostarda di frutta* is a gift from Cremona, across the Po River. Sweet and pungent fruits are cooked in a heavy syrup of sugar, corn syrup, vinegar, and mustard oil. The fruits are bottled and usually sold in 12-ounce jars. *Mostarda di frutta* may be found in specialty foods shops and Italian groceries.

SALSA VERDE

GREEN SAUCE
YIELDS ABOUT 1 CUP

Besides its importance as an accompaniment to *Bollito Misto*, this versatile condiment also is good as a dip with *crudités* or a sauce with boiled meats. The flavors are assertive but not overwhelming and can add interest even to a dish of simple boiled or steamed potatoes.

4 anchovies
1 tablespoon capers
1 gherkin or *cetriolino* (little cucumber)
2 tablespoons *pignoli* (pine nuts) or walnuts
1 small clove garlic (about ½ teaspoon), chopped
Green part of 1 scallion, thinly sliced
½ teaspoon dry mustard
½ cup chopped fresh parsley
Juice of ¼ lemon
⅓ to ½ cup olive oil
Freshly ground pepper

Pass the anchovies, capers, gherkin, nuts, and garlic through a fine grinder or finely chop in a food processor (do not over process). Put the mixture in a bowl and add the scallion. Stir in the mustard, parsley, lemon juice, olive oil, and pepper to taste.

La Bomba

La Bomba, the pride of the province, consists of rice formed into a hemisphere and filled with poultry. A guest unfulfilled with this dish causes embarassment to the host or hostess.

Every hamlet has its own version. My thrifty Zia Maria would use the meat of a chicken used to make broth, sauté it with herbs and vegetables, cover it with risotto and the sauce, and bake it. A friend of mine's aunt mixed chicken and tomato into the rice for a pink bomb. Nonna Vecchia cooked small pieces of chicken in with the rice and Nonno Giuseppe used game birds, in particular, quail. I often use Cornish game hens, and when I learned the original bird was the pigeon, I applauded myself.

> 2 Cornish game hens, cut into eighths
> ¼ cup flour
> 4 tablespoons butter
> I cup baby carrots, trimmed and cleaned
> I cup pearl onions, peeled
> 5 ounces fresh *porcini* or *cremini* mushrooms, trimmed and sliced
> ½ teaspoon dried sage
> 2 bay leaves
> ½ cup dry white wine
> I cup meat broth (page 65) or good-quality store-bought
> I recipe *risotto per pollame* (page 36)
> Salt and pepper
> ½ cup freshly grated Parmigiano-Reggiano

Rinse the hens, pat them dry, and dredge them in the flour. Heat the butter in a large sauté pan over medium heat and carefully add the game hens, skin side down. Add the carrots, onions, and mushrooms to the pan. When the hens are browned on all sides, add the sage, bay leaves, and wine. Bring the mixture to a boil, boil for 2 minutes, and add the broth. Cover the pan and simmer until the hens are tender. (This is a good time to start the risotto.) Remove the lid from the pan and reduce the cooking liquid to about three fourths of a cup.

Preheat the oven to 350° F.

La bomba may be presented undetonated. I prefer an exploding bomb.

To the cooked risotto add about ¼ cup of the sauce from cooking the hens and ¼ cup of the cheese. Butter a 3-quart bundt pan and press about half of the risotto into the bottom and along the sides. Put half of the meat into the pan and cover them with the remaining risotto. Bake the risotto for 30 minutes, remove the pan from the oven, and let the risotto rest for 5 or 10 minutes. Cover the pan with an ovenproof platter and turn *la bomba* out onto the platter. Put the remaining pieces of meat into the center of the molded risotto and pour the remaining sauce over all. Sprinkle the risotto with the remaining cheese and bake for 10 minutes. Serve *la bomba* at once.

A more conventional method is to press about half of the risotto into the bottom of a round ovenproof dish, bone the coooked hens, and place the meat in the middle of the dish. Cover the meat with the remaining risotto and follow the above procedure.

Tacchino Arrostito Ripieno di Castagne

Roast Turkey with Chestnut Stuffing

Serves 10

The stuffing is quite ancient, but the cooking of the American turkey is a relatively modern concept throughout Europe. Before the arrival of the turkey, the peacock was a festive delicacy.

4 tablespoons butter

Liver from the turkey, finely chopped

½ cup chopped onion

1 scallion, sliced

2½ quarts cubed 1- or 2-day-old bread

½ cup dry white wine

2 cups milk

2 cups cooked and peeled chesnuts (see note)

½ pound very fresh *mascarpone* or other soft cheese

⅔ cup freshly grated Parmigiano-Reggiano

1 teaspoon freshly grated nutmeg

3 extra-large eggs

Salt and pepper

1 (12- to 14-pound) turkey, cleaned

Preheat the oven to 425° F. Heat the butter in a sauté pan. Add the liver, onion, and scallions and sauté until soft and cooked through. Put the bread in a large bowl and pour in the wine and milk. Break each chestnut into 2 or 3 pieces and add them, with the cheeses and nutmeg, to the bread. Add the liver mixture, eggs, and salt and pepper to taste and mix thoroughly. Fill the front and rear cavities of the turkey with the stuffing (do not over-pack). Truss the turkey with butcher's twine or long wooden toothpicks.

Put the turkey on a rack in a roasting pan and roast it for 30 to 40 minutes, or until it begins to brown. Lower the temperature to 325° F. and roast for 4½ to 5 hours. When the turkey is done, the leg joints will move easily and the juice from the joints will run clear.

Note: To remove skins from chestnuts, bring a large pot of water to a boil. Slit the shells of the chesnuts, add them to the water, and cook for about 8 minutes, or until tender. Cool the chestnuts until they can be handled, then peel away the shells.

CAPPONE ARROSTITO RIPIENO DI SPINACI

ROASTED CAPON WITH SPINACH STUFFING

SERVES 8

Our favorite roasted bird with our favorite stuffing. It is delightful year round, and always served on Christmas day at our house.

1 (6-pound) capon

3 pounds fresh spinach or 3 (10-ounce) packages frozen spinach

2 cups 1-inch-cubed day-old white Italian bread

¼ cup milk

3 tablespoons butter

Liver from capon, finely chopped

4 scallions, finely sliced

4 to 6 ounces very fresh *mascarpone* or other soft cheese

½ cup freshly grated Parmigiano-Reggiano

2 eggs, lightly beaten

½ teaspoon dried basil

Salt and pepper

6 small white onions, cleaned and peeled

2 cups chicken broth (page 64) or good-quality store-bought

Rinse the capon under cold water and pat dry. Bring about 3 cups water to a rolling boil. If using fresh spinach, trim the tough stems and bruised leaves and wash the remaining leaves thoroughly. Add the spinach to the boiling water and cook until wilted, about 3 minutes. Immediately refresh the spinach in cold water. Drain the spinach, squeezing out as much excess water as possible, and chop it medium fine.

Put the bread in a large bowl, pour in the milk, and toss to combine. Heat the butter in a sauté pan, add the liver and scallions, and cook until the liver is no longer pink, adjusting the heat and taking care not to burn the liver or the scallions. Cook the liver until well done.

Preheat the oven to 450° F.

To the bread add the spinach, liver mixture, cheeses, eggs, basil, and salt and pepper to taste, and mix to combine well. Fill the front and the rear cavities of the capon with the stuffing (do not over-pack). Truss the capon with butcher's twine or long wooden toothpicks.

(continued)

Put a rack in a roasting pan and pour in the broth to a level of about ½ inch. Add the onions to bottom of pan. Put the capon on the rack and put the pan in the oven. Roast the capon 30 minutes, lower the oven temperature to 325° F., and roast the capon until it is golden brown, about 3½ hours. When the capon is done, the joints will move easily and the liquid from the joints will run clear.

Trota all'Aceto Rosso

Trout and Red-Wine Vinegar

SERVES 2

When my son Joseph and his fishing buddy Angelo bring home freshwater trout or bass, I cook it this way. Angelo always says, "This is the best fish ever."

2 (1-pound) whole trout, pan-ready
½ cup flour
⅓ cup olive oil
¼ cup red-wine vinegar
2 tablespoons chopped fresh parsley
2 tablespoons ¼-inch-thick slices of scallions

Dredge the trout in the flour. Heat the oil in a sauté pan over medium heat, carefully add the trout, and brown it on both sides. Pour the vinegar over the trout and let it sizzle for 30 to 40 seconds. Top the trout with the parsley and scallion and let it sizzle for 10 to 15 more seconds. To serve, pour the pan juices over the trout.

PESCE GATTO AL FORNO

BAKED CATFISH

SERVES 4

Whenever Dad's buddy Maurizio would catch a bullhead, Dad was ecstatic. Sometimes Nonno Guiseppe, who also liked them, would send his nephew Eddie fishing for bullheads, and the two of them would enjoy an intimate fish dinner. The more common name of this fish is catfish—*pesce gatto*, which in Italy are found in the Po River.

1 cup bread crumbs

1 scallion, finely sliced, or an equal amount of chives

¼ cup chopped onion

1 tablespoon chopped fresh basil

1 teaspoon chopped fresh thyme

1 tablespoon chopped fresh parsley

¼ cup olive oil

Salt and pepper

4 tablespoons butter

2 pounds catfish fillet

Preheat the oven to 375° F.

Put the bread crumbs, scallion, onion, herbs, oil, and salt and pepper in a bowl and mix well. Melt the butter in a roasting pan or on a baking sheet. Put the catfish in the melted butter and cover it with the breading. Bake the catfish until the breading is browned, about 20 minutes, or until the fish flakes easily (do not overcook).

CARPA CON ERBE AROMATICHE

CARP IN HERBS

SERVES 6

1 (3 pound) carp cut into 6 (8-ounce) fillets
¾ cup dry white wine
Juice of 1 lemon
1 scallion, sliced
2 tablespoons coarsely chopped fresh basil
2 tablespoons coarsely chopped fresh sage
2 tablespoons coarsely chopped fresh thyme
2 tablespoons chopped fresh parsley
Salt and pepper
4 tablespoons olive oil

Marinate the carp in the wine, lemon juice, scallion, herbs, and salt and pepper to taste for at least 30 minutes and up to 3 hours.

Preheat the oven to 375° F.

Heat the oil in a roasting pan in the oven. Add the carp with the marinade and bake until the carp is flaky and browned on top, about 20 minutes.

VERDURE

*I*n Parma, as elsewhere in Italy, vegetables are highly regarded for their gastronomic as well as nutritive qualities and are carefully prepared. Any and all preparations can be found in Parma's vegetable repertoire, from raw to braised, sautéed, baked, fried, grilled, and stuffed. Parma's fine soil yields a rich and varied crop on the plains as well as in the mountains. The legendary mushrooms of Borgo Val di Taro, in particular, are plentiful and are used both fresh and dried in countless dishes.

Vegetables, known as verdure, legumi, *or* contorni, *in the sense that they surround the entrée, may appear at any point in a meal. They can come before, during, or even after the main course. Salads are almost always included, usually following the main course. Although some salads can begin the meal, a simple green salad more typically comes at the end. More than one salad, particularly in summer, is quite acceptable.*

ZUCCHINI RIPIENI

Large zucchini are excellent for an entrée, and small ones make an ideal hot antipasto or an accompaniment to a main course. This versatile filling may also be used for stuffed eggplants or peppers.

2 (1-foot-long) zucchini, 2 inches or more in diameter
½ ounce dried *porcini* mushrooms
½ cup Marsala
8 tablespoons butter or ¼ cup olive oil
1 medium eggplant
1 medium onion, chopped
2 scallions, trimmed and thinly sliced
¼ to ½ cup dry bread crumbs
⅓ cup *pignoli* nuts (optional)
½ cup freshly grated Parmigiano-Reggiano
Salt and pepper

Preheat the oven to 375° F. Cut the zucchini in half lengthwise and remove the seeds from the centers. Leaving ⅛-inch-thick shells, scoop out the flesh with a spoon and reserve shells. Dice the flesh. Break up the dried mushrooms and soak them in the Marsala to soften.

Heat the butter in a large sauté pan over medium heat. Peel and dice the eggplant. When the butter is melted, add the eggplant, onion, and scallions. Drain the softened mushrooms, reserving the soaking liquid, and add them to the pan. When the eggplant is *al dente* add the zucchini to the pan. When the zucchini begin to soften, add the reserved soaking liquid and simmer about 1 minute. When the zucchini are *al dente*, remove the pan from the heat and add enough bread crumbs to bind the ingredients together. Add the *pignoli*, ⅓ cup of the cheese, and salt and pepper to taste.

Stuff the reserved zucchini shells with the filling and put in a baking dish or casserole. Add 1 cup of water to the baking dish and top the stuffed zucchini with the remaining cheese. Bake the zucchini in the oven for about 45 minutes, or until the filling is browned and the shells are *al dente*.

Note: The zucchini may be filled 2 to 3 days in advance and refrigerated, unbaked and covered. Add the water to the pan just before serving.

Zucchini e Funghi con Aceto

Zucchini and Mushrooms with Vinegar

Serves 4

¼ cup olive oil

5 ounces fresh cultivated white or *cremini* mushrooms

4 medium zucchini (about 1 pound)

2 tablespoons red-wine vinegar

Salt and pepper

Heat the oil in a large sauté pan over low heat. Clean and slice the mushrooms and carefully add them to the hot oil. Clean and slice the zucchini and add them to the pan. When the zucchini are *al dente* and just beginning to brown, stir in the vinegar and salt and pepper to taste. Raise the heat to medium-high and let the mixture sizzle about 15 seconds. Serve at once.

Zucchini alla Parmigiana

Zucchini Parmesan

Serves 4

Simplicity itself, this preparation also is elegant, and often accompanies roasted or grilled meats.

4 medium zucchini (about 1 pound)

¼ cup freshly grated Parmigiano-Reggiano

3 tablespoons butter, melted

Preheat the oven to 350°F. and bring a pot of water to a boil.

Clean the zucchini and cut them into 3-inch-long pieces. Cut each piece in half lengthwise. Add the zucchini to the boiling water and boil gently for 5 minutes. Drain the zucchini, pat them dry, and put them on a baking sheet, cut side up. Sprinkle the cheese evenly over the zucchini and drizzle the butter over the cheese. Note: The zucchini may be prepared to this point up to 1 day before baking.

Bake the zucchini in the oven until the cheese melts and begins to brown, about 15 minutes.

ABOUT GREENS

It is an old Parmesan belief that green vegetables build strong, healthy bodies and modern medical science bears this out.

All leafy green vegetables can be prepared for cooking according to a basic method. Cut off the stems and roots. Fill a sink with cold water and a little salt and add the greens. Lift the greens out of the water and shake them to remove any sand or grit as well as excess water. Repeat this procedure 2 more times or as necessary.

Put 3 inches of water and a pinch of salt in a large pot and bring the water to a rolling boil. Add the greens to the boiling water and cook, covered, until they are just past the wilted stage. Put the greens in a strainer or colander and chill under cold water to stop the cooking. Cooking times will vary with different greens and their age. Check the greens often, turning them, to avoid overcooking.

SPINACI ALLA PARMIGIANA

CREAMED SPINACH PARMESAN STYLE

SERVES 4

1 pound fresh spinach or 1 (10-ounce) package frozen spinach
4 tablespoons butter
2 tablespoons flour
1 teaspoon freshly grated nutmeg
⅓ cup milk
¼ cup freshly grated Parmigiano-Reggiano
Salt and pepper

If using fresh spinach, prepare it according to the basic method (see above). Chop the spinach.

Heat the butter in a sauce pan over medium heat and add the spinach. Stir in the flour and cook the mixture for 2 minutes; add the nutmeg. Slowly add the milk, stirring over low to medium heat for 6 or 7 minutes, until the mixture becomes creamy. Stir in the cheese and salt and pepper to taste.

FLAN DI SPINACI ALLA PARMIGIANO

*SPINACH SOUFFLÉ
PARMESAN STYLE*

SERVES 8 TO 10

I like to make this in a ring mold and fill the center with a simple carrot preparation (page 137).

4 pounds fresh spinach or 4 (10-ounce) packages frozen spinach

4 tablespoons butter

1 medium onion, chopped

2 tablespoons flour

1½ teaspoons freshly grated nutmeg

1 cup milk

4 ounces very fresh *mascarpone* or other soft cheese

¾ cup freshly grated Parmigiano-Reggiano

3 eggs, lightly beaten

Salt and pepper

Preheat the oven to 400° F. Butter a 2-quart ring mold.

If using fresh spinach, prepare it according to the basic method (page 123). Chop the spinach.

Heat the butter in a pot and sauté the onion until translucent and glazed. Mix in the flour and cook until the mixture is smooth, about 2 minutes. Blend in the nutmeg and slowly pour in the milk while stirring. Bring the mixture to a slow boil and cook until it is thick enough to coat the back of a spoon. Remove the pot from the heat and let it cool slightly. Mix in the spinach, cheeses, eggs, and salt and pepper to taste.

Put the mixture in the ring mold. Put the ring mold in a baking pan and add enough hot water to come about two thirds up the side of the mold. Bake the soufflé for about 1 hour and 15 minutes, or until a large toothpick plunged into the soufflé comes out clean. Let the mold rest for a few minutes and turn the soufflé out onto a serving platter.

BIETOLE AL BURRO E LIMONE

Swiss Chard with Butter and Lemon

SERVES 4 TO 6

1½ pounds Swiss chard
3 tablespoons butter
Straned juice of 1 lemon
Salt and pepper

Prepare Swiss chard according to the basic method (page 123). Drain the Swiss chard in a strainer or colander and squeeze dry. Heat the butter in a large sauté pan over medium heat and add the chard. Drizzle the chard with the lemon juice and heat thoroughly. Season the chard with salt and pepper to taste and serve hot.

BARBABIETOLE E CIME DI BARBABIETOLE

Beets and Beet Greens

SERVES 4

*T*his delicious, aromatic vegetable dish compliments most entrées and is highly nutritious. If you can only find beets without their greens, spinach or Swiss chard can be substituted.

1 pound young (small to medium) beets with their greens, scrubbed but not peeled
3 tablespoons butter
3 scallions, trimmed and sliced ¼ inch thick
Strained juice of 1 lemon
Salt and pepper

Remove the beet greens and carefully clean both the beets and greens.

Bring a medium pot of water to a boil, add the beets and boil until they are fork-tender, 20 to 30 minutes, depending on their size. Drain the beets and put them in cold water until cool enough to handle. To peel the beets, cover them with a paper towel or plastic wrap and rub the skin off.

Cook the beet greens according to the basic method (page 123). Coarsely chop the greens and dice the beets. Heat the butter in a large sauté pan over medium heat and add the scallions. When the scallions are soft, add the beets and greens and cook them until hot. Add the lemon juice and salt and pepper to taste. Serve hot.

FUNGHI RIPIENI AL FORNO

We serve stuffed mushrooms with most roasts or as a warm antipasto. With an assortment of other vegetable dishes, stuffed or not, they can be part of a satisfying meatless entrée.

10 ounces fresh cultivated white or *cremini* mushrooms, about the size of silver dollars
4 tablespoons butter
½ medium onion, chopped
1 scallion, trimmed and thinly sliced
½ to ¾ cup dried bread crumbs
½ cup freshly grated Parmigiano-Reggiano
2 teaspoons chopped fresh parsley

Preheat the oven to 400° F.

Clean the mushrooms and gently pull the stems from the caps, reserving the stems and leaving the mushrooms hollowed out. Heat the butter in a sauté pan over medium heat and sauté the onion and scallion, stirring occasionally. Chop the reserved mushroom stems. When the onion and scallion are soft, add the stems, cook until they are just *al dente*, and remove the pan from the heat. Add the bread crumbs, cheese, and parsley and stir to combine.

Stuff the mushroom caps with the filling and bake on a baking sheet until golden brown, about 20 minutes.

Note: The stuffed mushrooms can be refrigerated for up to 2 days or frozen and baked later.

MELANZANE RIPIENE AL FORNO

BAKED STUFFED
EGGPLANT
SERVES 4

The meatiness of eggplant, along with its versatility, makes it one of the most useful of all vegetables. Here it makes for an inexpensive meal that is high in nutrition.

2 large eggplants (about 1½ to 2 pounds)

¼ cup olive oil

2 medium onions

1 large clove garlic, chopped

4 medium zucchini (about 1 pound)

1 (28-ounce) can plum tomatoes, drained

1 tablespoon whole dried basil

1 teaspoon whole dried oregano

1 teaspoon dried thyme

¼ cup chopped fresh parsley

½ cup freshly grated Parmigiano-Reggiano

Salt and pepper

Preheat the oven to 400° F. Cut the eggplants in half lengthwise. Leaving ⅛-inch-thick shells, scoop out the flesh with a spoon and reserve shells. Cut the flesh into ½-inch pieces.

Heat the oil in a large sauté pan over medium heat. Slice the onions. Carefully add the eggplants, onions, and garlic to the hot oil. Clean the zucchini and cut them into ¼-inch dice. When the eggplants are soft, add the zucchini. Break or cut the tomatoes into 1-inch pieces and add them to the pan. When the zucchini begin to soften, stir in the herbs and simmer for about 1 minute. Remove the pan from the heat and stir in ⅓ cup of the cheese and salt and pepper to taste. Stuff the reserved eggplant shells with the filling and sprinkle the remaining cheese over the tops. Put the eggplants on a baking sheet or in a shallow baking dish and bake for 45 minutes to 1 hour or until the tops begin to brown and the shells are *al dente*.

Note: The filled eggplants can be refrigerated for up to 2 days or frozen and baked later.

OVERLEAF, CLOCKWISE
FROM RIGHT: *Sautéed
Fennel and Peas, Beets and
Beet Greens, Baked Rice-
Stuffed Peppers, Baked
Stuffed Mushrooms, Baked
Stuffed Eggplant, Stuffed
Zucchini, Asparagus
Parmesan Style, Salad of
Savoy Cabbage and Beans*

PEPERONI RIPIENI DI RISO AL FORNO

Baked Rice-Stuffed Peppers

SERVES 8

We always serve this as an entrée. Sometimes I prepare a tomato mushroom sauce (page 59) with the peppers. When the sauce is half-cooked, I add it to the baking dish instead of the water or other options given below.

1½ cups long-grain rice
10 tablespoons butter
½ medium onion
1 scallion, thinly sliced
1 medium zucchini, cleaned and diced
½ cup new peas (fresh or frozen)
⅓ cup milk
2 eggs, lightly beaten
4 ounces very fresh *mascarpone* or other soft cheese
⅔ cup freshly grated Parmigiano-Reggiano
Salt and pepper
8 red, yellow, and/or green bell peppers, wiped clean
2 cups water, broth (page 64 or 65) or good-quality store-bought, meat essence, or half-cooked tomato mushroom sauce (page 59)

Preheat the oven to 350° F.

Steam or boil the rice until it is just *al dente* and reserve, uncovered.

Heat the butter in a large sauté pan, add the onion and scallion, and cook until soft. Combine the reserved rice, onion mixture, zucchini, peas, milk, eggs, cheeses, and salt and pepper to taste.

Cut around the stems of the peppers to remove the tops and reserve the tops. Remove the cores and excess membrane from the peppers, taking care not to pierce them. Stuff the peppers with the rice filling and cover them with the pepper caps.

Put the stuffed peppers in a baking dish with the water or other liquid and bake in the oven until the peppers are tender, 45 minutes to 1 hour.

Note: The peppers may be filled a day in advance of baking, and kept, covered, in the refrigerator.

POMODORI RIPIENI AL FORNO

BAKED STUFFED TOMATOES

SERVES 6

Serve these as an accompaniment to roasted meat, as a first course, or as part of a light lunch.

6 ripe but firm medium tomatoes
½ cup dry bread crumbs
½ cup chopped fresh parsley
1 tablespoon coursely chopped fresh basil (optional)
1 scallion, trimmed and thinly sliced
½ tablespoon olive oil
¼ cup freshly grated Parmigiano-Reggiano
Salt and pepper

Preheat the oven to 350° F.

Cut the tops off the tomatoes and remove the cores and seeds. Combine the bread crumbs, parsley, basil, scallion, oil, cheese, and salt and pepper to taste in a bowl and mix well. Divide the filling among the tomatoes, put them in a shallow baking dish and bake in the oven until the tomatoes are heated through but remain firm, about 10 minutes.

Note: The tomatoes can be made 3 to 4 hours in advance.

ABOUT ASPARAGUS

Choose asparagus with firm, bright-green stems and closed dark buds on the tips. Keep them in a cold section of the refrigerator. (If possible, stand the asparagus stalks upright in water or lying down with a little ice on them.) Treat asparagus delicately to avoid damaging the stalks. To prepare asparagus for cooking, gently run cold water over the stalks to remove any sand and trim the ends. The thickest asparagus stalks must be peeled before cooking, so that the tips and the stems reach the *al dente* stage at the same time.

As a kitchen apprentice, I learned to cook asparagus tied in small bundles and boiled. My mother cooked asparagus in an espresso pot. She put the stem ends in boiling water in the upside-down pot and covered the tips with the bottom of the pot, and would then boil the stems and steam the tips. Asparagus also can be steamed.

ASPARAGI ALLA PARMIGIANA

ASPARAGUS PARMESAN STYLE

SERVES 6

For Parmigiani, there is a celebratory feeling about asparagus, and this preparation is the absolute favorite, especially in early Spring.

I pound asparagus, cleaned
⅓ cup freshly grated Parmigiano-Reggiano
4 tablespoons butter, melted
Freshly ground pepper

Preheat the oven to 375° F.

Put ¼ inch of water and a large pinch of salt in a large sauté pan and bring the water to a boil, covered. Add the asparagus to the boiling water and cover. Cook pencil-thin asparagus for about 2 minutes and thick Colossal stalks for about 8 minutes. The asparagus should be tender inside but still crisp. Carefully drain the asparagus and refresh under ice water.

Arrange the asparagus on an ovenproof platter, sprinkle the cheese over the tips, and drizzle the butter over all. Season the asparagus with the pepper to taste and bake in the oven until the cheese begins to brown, about 5 minutes.

ASPARAGI AL BURRO E LIMONE

◆▶◆▶◆▶◆▶◆▶◆▶◆▶

ASPARAGUS IN
BUTTER AND LEMON

SERVES 6

A delicate, classic vegetable dish that takes 15 minutes, this can accompany an entrée, meat, or fish, or be served as a simple first course.

1 pound asparagus, cleaned
3 tablespoons butter
Strained juice of 1 lemon
Salt and pepper

Cook asparagus according to the method for *Asparagi alla Parmigiana* (page 132). Heat the butter in a sauté pan over medium heat and add the asparagus. Drizzle the asparagus with the lemon juice and let it sizzle briefly. Season the asparagus with the salt and pepper to taste and serve hot.

BROCCOLI ALLA PARMIGIANA

◆▶◆▶◆▶◆▶◆▶◆▶◆▶

BROCCOLI
PARMESAN STYLE

SERVES 6

1 bunch broccoli
⅓ cup freshly grated Parmigiano-Reggiano
4 tablespoons butter, melted
Salt and pepper

Preheat the oven to 375° F.

Separate the broccoli into florets, leaving 1½ inches of stem on each, discard any discolored areas, and rinse gently. Put ¼ inch of water and a large pinch of salt in a large sauté pan and bring the water to a boil, covered. Add the broccoli to the boiling water and cook, covered, for 5 to 6 minutes. The broccoli should be tender inside but still crisp. Carefully drain the broccoli and refresh under ice water. Arrange the broccoli on an ovenproof platter with the florets all facing in the same direction. Sprinkle the broccoli with the cheese and drizzle with some butter. Season the broccoli with the salt and pepper to taste and bake in the oven until the cheese melts and begins to brown.

PUREA DI PATATE AL FORNO ALLA PARMIGIANA

Baked Mashed Potatoes Parmesan Style

SERVES 4 TO 6

*T*his great potato preparation from Parma's Apennine mountains varies from hamlet to hamlet. Some cooks add a little nutmeg and fresh basil or thyme. Others use onions or scallions—or both—or chives. Garlic is never used, as it masks the flavors. This is my favorite recipe for this traditional dish.

> 1½ pounds Maine or Eastern potatoes, scrubbed but not peeled
> 4 tablespoons butter
> ¼ cup chopped onion
> ⅓ cup chopped leek
> ½ cup milk
> ⅓ cup plus I tablespoon freshly grated Parmigiano-Reggiano
> Salt and pepper

Preheat the oven to 375° F.

Bring a medium to large pot of water to a boil and add the potatoes. While the potatoes are cooking, heat the butter in a small skillet, add the onion and leek, and sauté until the onions are translucent.

Peel the cooked potatoes and pass them through a ricer. Stir in the milk with a whisk or wooden spoon and mix in the onion, leeks, ⅓ cup of the cheese, and salt and pepper to taste. Turn the potato mixture out into a buttered I-quart baking dish and sprinkle the remaining cheese over the top. Bake the potatoes in the oven until the top begins to brown, about 30 minutes.

Note: This dish may be prepared a day in advance and refrigerated, covered. Remove the potatoes from the refrigerator about I hour before baking.

PATATE ARROSTITE CON ERBE AROMATICHE

ROAST POTATOES WITH AROMATIC HERBS

SERVES 6

*T*he delicate balance of herbs in this preparation connects the potatoes with most other dishes for just about any occasion. Roast meats of all kinds have an affinity to the tastes within—I cannot recall ever serving roast pork without these succulent potatoes.

> 2 pounds red new potatoes, scrubbed but not peeled
> 3 tablespoons olive oil
> 1 teaspoon dried basil or 1 tablespoon chopped fresh basil
> 1 teaspoon dried rosemary or 1 tablespoon chopped fresh rosemary
> 1 teaspoon dried thyme or 1 tablespoon chopped fresh thyme
> ¼ cup trimmed and thinly sliced scallions or chives
> Salt and pepper

Preheat the oven to 400° F.

Cut the potatoes to the size of walnuts. (If the potatoes are very small, leave them whole.) Put the potatoes in a baking dish with the oil, herbs, scallions and salt and pepper to taste, turning and stirring the potatoes to evenly coat them with the oil and seasonings. Roast the potatoes in the oven until they are tender, about 1 hour.

Insalata di Patate e Peperoni

Potato and Pepper Salad

Serves 6 to 8

One of our scrumptious potato salads. Ideal with a light entrée or as part of a cookout. Whole small red new potatoes can be used in place of the larger sliced ones, and capers can be a delightful addition.

2 pounds russet potatoes

½ medium red onion

1 sweet red bell pepper

2 tablespoons chopped fresh parsley

2 tablespoons chopped fresh basil

4 tablespoons olive oil

1 tablespoon red-wine vinegar

2 tablespoons mayonnaise

Salt and pepper

Peel and boil the potatoes. When the cooked potatoes are cool enough to handle, slice them about ⅛-inch thick. Cut the onion into very thin slices. Clean, core, and seed the pepper and cut it lengthwise into ⅛-inch slices. Put all the vegetables in a salad bowl and sprinkle them with the herbs. Whisk together the oil, vinegar, mayonnaise, and salt and pepper to taste then dress the salad, taking care not to break up the potatoes.

CAROTE

A simple vegetable dish I like to serve whenever I serve *Flan di Spinaci alla Parmigiana*—spinach soufflé—(page 124). It is a pretty dish.

I pound medium carrots or baby carrots
4 tablespoons butter
I medium onion
½ teaspoon sugar
I tablespoon chopped fresh parsley
Salt and pepper

If using medium carrots, wash and peel them and slice ⅛-inch thick on a 45° angle. If using baby carrots, leave them whole and wash but do not peel them. Bring ¼ inch of lightly salted water to boil in a saucepan, add the carrots, and cook until they are barely tender. Drain the carrots. Heat the butter in a sauté pan. Slice the onion about ¼ inch thick and add to the pan. When the onions are half-cooked, add the carrots and cook until the onions are translucent. Stir in the sugar, parsley, and salt and pepper to taste. Serve hot.

FINOCCHIO BRASATO

❦❦❦❦❦❦❦❦❦

BRAISED FENNEL

SERVES 4

I medium fennel bulb

4 tablespoons butter

½ cup meat broth (page 65) or good-quality store-bought

I tablespoon chopped fresh parsley

Salt and pepper

Wash and trim the fennel bulb, reserving about I tablespoon of the fennel fronds, and cut it into 8 wedges. Heat the butter in a large sauté pan over medium heat and add the fennel wedges. Sauté the fennel on all sides until it begins to brown, about 3 minutes. Pour the broth over the fennel and bring it to a slow boil. Cook the fennel until it is *al dente* and reduce the liquid until only about ⅛ inch of it remains. Sprinkle the fennel with the parsley and reserved fennel fronds and season with the salt and pepper to taste. Put the fennel in a serving dish and pour the pan juices over it. Serve hot.

FINOCCHIO E PISELLI IN PADELLA

❦❦❦❦❦❦❦❦❦

SAUTÉED FENNEL AND PEAS

SERVES 4

I medium fennel bulb

4 tablespoons butter

½ tablespoon flour

I tablespoons chives

½ cup meat broth (page 65) or good-quality store-bought

5 ounces new peas (fresh or frozen)

Salt and pepper

Wash and trim the fennel bulb, reserving about 2 tablespoons of the fennel fronds, and cut it into 8 wedges. Heat the butter in a large sauté pan over medium heat and add the fennel wedges. Sauté the fennel until it is browned lightly on all sides, about 3 minutes. Remove the fennel from the pan and stir the flour into the butter. Cook the roux, stirring, until it is light brown, taking care not to let it burn. Stir in the chives and broth and bring the mixture to a slow boil. Return the fennel to the pan, add the peas, and cook the vegetables until they are *al dente*, about 5 minutes. Add the reserved fennel fronds and salt and pepper to taste, cook for 40 more seconds, and put on an oval platter. Serve hot.

INSALATA DI FINOCCHIO E SEDANO

FENNEL AND
CELERY SALAD
SERVES 4

*T*his is a light, low-calorie dish to start a meal, or a great way to end one with the addition of a little wedge of cheese—young Parmigiano-Reggiano would be perfect. When served as an antipasto, the tomatoes are omitted, but black olives may be added.

½ bunch celery, washed and outer ribs discarded
½ medium fennel bulb, washed
½ sweet red pepper
3 plum tomatoes (optional)
I tablespoon chopped chives or green part of a scallion
¼ cup olive oil
Strained juice of I lemon
Salt and pepper

Peel off any stringy fibers from the celery and fennel. Trim both vegetables, reserving 2 tablespoons each of celery leaves and fennel fronds. Slice the vegetables lengthwise very thinly and cut into I-inch-long pieces. Clean, core, and seed the pepper and slice it very thinly. Wash and slice the tomatoes into thin wedges. Put all the vegetables in a salad bowl.

Chop the reserved celery leaves and fennel fronds and add them to the salad with the chives. Drizzle the oil and lemon juice over the salad and season with the salt and pepper to taste. Toss salad to combine well. Let the salad marinate in the refrigerator, covered, for 3 to 5 hours.

Insalata di Cavolo di Savoia e Fagioli

Salad of Savoy Cabbage and Beans

SERVES 6

*T*his salad is often served as a main course, particularly on hot summer days. It also is a nice addition to a picnic or buffet.

½ cup dried roman beans, soaked overnight and drained

½ cup dried small white beans, soaked overnight and drained

1½ to 2 pounds Savoy cabbage, shredded

¼ cup finely diced celery

½ cup thinly sliced red onion

¼ cup chopped fresh basil

½ teaspoon finely minced garlic

Strained juice of 2 lemons

Salt and pepper

Bring a large pot of water to a boil and add the beans. Simmer the beans, covered, for 2 hours or until they are tender but not mushy, adding additional water if necessary. Drain the beans and refresh them under cold water. Put all the ingredients in a salad bowl, adding the salt and pepper to taste, and toss to combine well. Let the salad marinate in the refrigerator for at least 30 minutes and up to 6 hours before serving.

Nonna Vecchia's Insalata di Savoia per la Buona Salute

Great-Grandmother's Health Slaw

SERVES 4

*T*his was my family's favorite salad. Whenever anyone dropped in to visit, there was always a bowl of Nonna's health slaw ready to be eaten.

½ pound Savoy cabbage, shredded

½ cup sliced celery with leaves

1 scallion, trimmed and thinly sliced

1 medium tomato, diced

½ cucumber, peeled and diced

⅓ cup olive oil

Strained juice of ½ lemon

2 tablespoons red-wine vinegar

Salt and pepper

Put all the vegetables in a salad bowl. Add the oil, lemon juice, vinegar, and salt and pepper to taste and toss to combine well. Let the salad marinate in the refrigerator for at least 30 minutes and up to 6 hours before serving.

FLAN DI ZUCCA

WINTER SQUASH SOUFFLÉ

SERVES 6

1 (2-pound) butternut squash or pumpkin

4 ounces very fresh *mascarpone* or other soft cheese

½ cup freshly grated Parmigiano-Reggiano

3 tablespoons potato or wheat flour

½ teaspoon freshly grated nutmeg

2 eggs, lightly beaten

Salt and pepper

Preheat the oven to 400° F.

Steam, prick the skin and bake, or microwave the squash and peel and seed it when it is cool enough to handle. Pass the squash through a ricer. Reserve 1 tablespoon of the Parmigiano-Reggiano and mix in the flour, nutmeg, and eggs. Season the squash mixture with the salt and pepper to taste. Spoon the squash mixture into a buttered 1-quart souffle dish, top with the reserved cheese, and bake in the oven for 50 minutes to 1 hour or until the soufflé is golden brown and firm.

INSALATA DI BARBABIETOLE E PATATE

Beet and Potato Salad

SERVES 6

½ pound red new potatoes, scrubbed but not peeled

½ pound small beets, scrubbed but not peeled

7 tablespoons olive oil

½ cup thinly sliced celery with leaves

½ cup loosely packed red onion slices

2 tablespoons red-wine vinegar

1 tablespoon chopped fresh parsley

Salt and pepper

Bring a pot of water to a boil and boil the potatoes until they are tender, about 20 minutes. Set them aside until cool enough to handle. Cook and peel the beets according to the method for *Barbabietole e Cime di Barbabietole* (page 125).

Heat the oil in a large sauté pan over medium heat. Carefully add the potatoes, beets, celery, and onion and cook the vegetables, stirring gently, just until they are hot, about 5 minutes. Add the vinegar, parsley, and salt and pepper to taste and combine gently. Serve warm or at room temperature.

Insalata di Cicoria di Campo con Uova

Dandelion and Egg Salad

SERVES 4

*T*his salad is loaded with nutrients. It is excellent with a light meal or as a main course salad. When gathering wild dandelions, pick small, unflowered greens. Should dandelions be unavailable, arugula may be substituted.

½ pound small, tender dandelion greens or arugula

1 scallion, trimmed and thinly sliced

2 hard-boiled eggs, quartered

4 tablespoons olive oil

1½ teaspoons red-wine vinegar

Salt and pepper

Trim the dandelion greens and wash the leaves thoroughly according to the basic method (page 123).

Put the greens, scallion, and eggs in a salad bowl and dress with the oil and vinegar. Season the salad with salt and pepper to taste.

INSALATA DI INDIVIA RICCIA

CHICORY SALAD

SERVES 6

½ pound chicory

1 slice red onion

½ sweet red bell pepper julienne

½ cup thinly sliced mushrooms

½ cucumber, peeled and cut into 2-inch wedges

3 tablespoons shredded carrot

3 tablespoons shredded radish

2 semi-hard-boiled eggs (boiled about 10 minutes)

3 plum tomatoes, cut into wedges

⅓ cup olive oil

2 tablespoons red-wine vinegar

Salt and pepper

Wash and dry the chicory. Tear the chicory into 3-inch pieces, and put it into a large salad bowl. In the center of the chicory put the onion slice, separated into rings, the pepper, mushrooms, cucumbers, carrot, and radish. Cut the eggs into wedges and alternate wedges of eggs and tomatoes around the outer rim of the salad. Dress the salad with the oil and vinegar and season with the salt and pepper to taste.

INSALATA CAPRICCIOSA

MIXED RAW
VEGETABLES

SERVES 6 TO 8

*T*his is a pretty salad to follow a light meal or a soup or pasta entrée. With bread and cheese it is an easy lunch.

1 head Boston lettuce

½ head Romaine, dark green outer leaves discarded

½ sweet red or green bell pepper

2 thin slices red onion

½ cucumber

5 medium cultivated white mushrooms, trimmed and wiped or rinsed clean

5 radishes, trimmed and washed

2 plum tomatoes

¼ cup olive oil

1 ½ tablespoons red-wine vinegar

Salt and pepper

Wash and dry the lettuces thoroughly. Line a salad bowl with the Boston lettuce. Cut the light green and yellow leaves of the romaine into thirds and put them in the middle of the bowl. Clean, core, and seed the pepper and slice it very thin. Put the pepper on the romaine. Separate the onion slices into rings and scatter them over the pepper. Peel the cucumber, cut it into ½-inch wedges, and add to the salad. Slice the mushrooms and radishes and spread over the top. Cut the tomatoes into 6 wedges and put them around the outer rim of the salad. Bring the salad to the table, dress it with the oil and vinegar, and toss it just before serving.

Note: The salad may be made 3 hours in advance and kept, covered, in the refrigerator. Dress the salad just before serving.

Insalata di Lattuga Romana e Parmigiano

Romaine Lettuce and Shaved Parmigiano

SERVES 4

½ head romaine

1 sweet red bell pepper

4 slices red onion

1 (1-ounce) wedge Parmigiano-Reggiano

Strained juice of ½ lemon

2 tablespoons red-wine vinegar

⅓ cup olive oil

Salt and pepper

Wash and dry the romaine, cut it into thirds, and put it in a salad bowl. Clean, core, and seed the pepper and slice it lengthwise. Arrange the pepper over the lettuce. Separate the onion slices into rings and arrange over the lettuce. Shave the cheese over the salad using the 1-inch slots on a 4-sided grater.

Put the lemon juice into a small bowl and add the vinegar. Slowly add the oil while whipping with a fork or whisk (the dressing will thicken slightly). Season the dressing with the salt and pepper to taste, pour it over the salad, and toss to combine.

DOLCI

*W*hen I was growing up, our everyday meals most often ended with the fruit my mother baked in her kitchen. For fancier sweets, we had Nonno Conti's Italian French pastry shop and Camillo Restaurant. It was not until a holiday in Parma that I truly appreciated the Val Taro's desserts.

Engraved in my mind is that first experience: We were sitting in Nonno's little old farmhouse, which had a wood-burning cook stove and furnishings that were more than a hundred years old. A knock on the door disturbed the tranquil mood. A little person in a print dress, blond pigtails, and big blue eyes stood in the doorway. It was Anna Maria with her grandmother, Cousin Ida, who was in a brownish-gray medieval-styled garment and carried a golden brown cake dusted with powdered sugar.

Ida had baked us a welcome cake. To a young aspiring culinary artist, the cake at first glance lacked sophistication. A close look at a piece of Ida's cake revealed an unfamiliar color and texture; my first bite, a moist crumbly texture and a unique flavor. With my second piece, I asked Ida about the ingredients and preparation. To my surprise I learned that it was a plain potato cake.

So much for a young upstart New Yorker in the provinces.

IDA'S FOCACCIA DI FECOLA DI PATATE

*IDA'S POTATO
FLOUR CAKE*

MAKES 2 CAKES

When I returned from my holiday in Europe, I was determined to duplicate Cousin Ida's *Focaccia di Fecola di Patate*. Fortunately, I produced a perfect *focaccia* with my first attempt. This is a truly simple preparation for a light dessert that satisfies the sweet tooth.

8 tablespoons butter
1½ cups potato flour
1 tablespoons baking powder
Zest of 1 lemon
½ teaspoon salt
4 eggs
¾ cup granulated sugar
Powdered sugar

Preheat the oven to 350° F. and butter and flour two 9-inch baking pans.

Heat the butter in a saucepan over low heat and remove the pan from the heat as soon as the butter melts.

Put the flour, baking powder, lemon zest, and salt in a mixing bowl and mix well. Put the eggs and granulated sugar in another mixing bowl and with an electric mixer beat together until the mixture increases to about 4 times its volume and forms soft peaks. Continue beating and very slowly drizzle the melted butter into the egg mixture. Gently fold in the flour.

Pour the batter into the pans and bake the cakes in the oven for 30 minutes, or until a toothpick inserted in the center of each cake comes out clean. Turn the cakes out of the pans onto wire racks. When they are cool, dust the tops with the powdered sugar.

Torta Dolce di Sandra

Sandra's Potato Flour Cake

1 cup butter at room temperature

1 cup sugar

4 eggs

1 teaspoon vanilla extract

1¾ cups potato flour

½ teaspoon salt

1 tablespoon baking powder

Preheat the oven to 350° F. and butter and flour an 8- by 5- by 2⅔-inch loaf pan.

With an electric mixer, cream the butter in a mixing bowl. Add the sugar and beat until the mixture is light in color and fluffy. Continue beating and add the eggs, 2 at a time. Maintain a creamy consistency and add the vanilla extract. In another mixing bowl mix together the flour, salt, and baking soda and gently add to the butter mixture. Pour the batter into the pan and bake the cake in the oven for 45 minutes, or until a toothpick inserted in the center of each cake comes out clean. Turn the cake out of the pan onto a wire rack to cool.

Crostata di Ricotta

Cheesecake

FOR THE PASTRY:

3½ cups cake flour

3 tablespoons sugar

1 teaspoon salt

5 tablespoons vegetable shortening

5 tablespoons butter

2 extra-large egg yolks or 1 extra-large egg

4 tablespoons Amaretto di Saronno

½ cup golden raisins

2 pounds ricotta

½ cup sugar

1 tablespoon potato flour

2 teaspoons vanilla extract

½ teaspoon salt

Zest of 1 orange

1 tablespoon diced candied orange

1 tablespoon diced candied citron

½ cup blanched almonds or pignoli

3 extra-large eggs

To make the pastry: Put the dry ingredients into a mixing bowl. With your fingertips work the shortening and butter into the dry ingredients until pieces the size of cherries are formed. Lightly beat together the egg and Amaretto in a bowl and add to the flour mixture. Quickly combine and work into a smooth ball or dough, but take care not to overwork it. Put the dough in a cool area or the refrigerator to rest for at least 20 minutes and up to 1 or 2 days.

To make the filling: Soak the raisins in ½ cup of water.

Put the ricotta in a large mixing bowl and add the sugar, flour, vanilla extract, salt, and orange zest. Beat the mixture to combine well. Drain the raisins and add them to the ricotta mixture with the candied orange and citron. Fold in the almonds.

Preheat the oven to 400° F. and butter and flour a 9- by 3-inch spring-form pan.Roll out the dough to about ⅛ inch thick and transfer it to the pan. Put the pan in a cool area or the refrigerator.

Beat 2 eggs until they increase to about 4 times their volume and form soft peaks. Fold the eggs into the ricotta mixture and pour the batter into the pan. Cut away any excess dough and roll the dough ⅛ inch thick. With a ravioli cutter or knife, cut strips about ½ inch wide. Arrange the strips in a lattice pattern over the filling, pressing the strips to the edge of the dough lining the pan to seal. Make an egg wash by beating the remaining egg with 1 tablespoon of water. Using a small brush paint the top of the cheesecake with the egg wash. Bake the cheesecake in the oven until the top is golden brown, about 1 hour. The center should remain slightly moist.

TIRAMISÙ

◆▪▪▪▪▪▪▪▪▪▪◆

"PICK-ME-UP"

*I*t was about 1984 when a friend brought me a new *dolce* from Italy called *tiramisù*. I tasted it, and it brought back memories from my childhood. Zia used to make the same dessert for me. My friend said it was from Lombardy, and he said that the main ingredient was a new cheese called *mascarpone*.

Recently, I was discussing deserts with my cousin Sandra, and she said "Don't forget *tiramisù*—pick-me-up." I told her the dessert was from Lombardy. She responded "No-no-no Ricardo." She made me reconsider. All the *trattorie* and grocery stores in the province seem to serve *tiramisù*.

When Zia made this sweet, she put cream cheese in a bowl and when it was soft, she made it lighter and smoother by slowly pouring in milk and rapidly stirring with a wooden spoon. Then she added a few spoonfuls of sugar, coffee left over from breakfast, and a bit of chocolate. She would then beat a couple of egg whites, sweeten them, and fold them into the cream cheese mixture. She lined a pan or a dish with plain cake such as spongecake or pound cake, perhaps moisten it with a liqueur syrup, and then fill it with the cream cheese mixture. To firm the cake, Zia would set it on ice in her ice box for a few hours. Although Zia had a refrigerator, she kept the ice box until the ice man passed away.

Here is how my father at seventy-six years of age made *tiramisù*. His base was lady cake, not just fingers, a Camillo specialty.

FOR LADY CAKE:

 I cup cake flour
 ½ teaspoon salt
 9 eggs, separated
 I cup sugar
 I½ teaspoons vanilla extract

FOR THE FILLING:

 4 egg whites
 ¾ cup sugar
 2 ounces double-strength espresso
 ½ ounce coffee liqueur

I pound *mascarpone*

¾ cup heavy cream

1 ½ tablespoons sugar

1 teaspoon vanilla extract

To assemble:

1 ounce unsweetened chocolate

1 tablespoon granulated sugar

Preheat the oven to 350° F. and butter and flour a three 9- by 1-inch baking pans.

To make the cake: Sift the flour and salt together onto a sheet of wax paper. With an electric mixer beat the egg whites in a large bowl until they form stiff peaks. Beat the egg yolks, sugar, and vanilla extract in another large bowl until they are light in color, fluffy, and form soft peaks. Delicately fold the flour mixture, ⅓ at a time, into the yolk mixture and fold the egg whites, ⅓ at a time, into the yolk mixture. Pour the batter into the pans and bake the cake layers in the oven for 30 minutes, or until a toothpick inserted in the center of the cake layers comes out clean.

Cool the layers in the pans and turn them out onto wire racks. The layers may be prepared 1 day in advance and covered with plastic wrap.

To make the filling: With an electric mixer beat the egg whites in a large bowl until they form stiff peaks. Heat the sugar and espresso in a small saucepan over medium heat, boiling to dissolve the sugar and make a syrup. Immediately whisk the hot syrup into the egg whites and drizzle in the liqueur. Refrigerate the mixture to cool. Beat together the *mascarpone*, cream, sugar, and vanilla extract until the mixture forms soft peaks. Reserve ¼ cup of the mixture in the refrigerator. When the cooked meringue is cool, fold it into the *mascarpone* mixture.

To assemble the cake: Put 1 cake layer on a cake plate. Cover the layer with ¼ inch of coffee filling and shave about ½ tablespoon of chocolate over the filling. Continue layering the remaining cake layers and filling. Using a pastry bag fitted with a small star tip, decorate the edge of the cake with the reserved *mascarpone* mixture. Shave a light covering of the chocolate over the cake, and sprinkle with the sugar. The *tiramisù* may be made in advance and refrigerated overnight.

OVERLEAF, CLOCKWISE FROM TOP: *Chestnut Pudding, Tiramisù ("Pick-Me-Up"), Ice Cream Cake, Miniature Pastries, Pears Cooked in Red Wine*

LA FRUTTA COTTA
COOKED FRUIT

Without a doubt, cooked fruits were among my mother's specialties. Though she never said so, we think she learned her techniques from her grandmother, Nonna Vecchia, and her father-in-law, Nonno Giuseppe. In spite of my mother's secrecy, through perseverance and Dad's sly eye we were able to reproduce some great fruit dishes and pass them along.

For the best results, always buy fruits that are beginning to ripen but are still too hard to eat. I prefer to leave the skin on whenever possible because it is loaded with nutrients, including pectin, which is thought to be effective in lowering cholesterol. To remove the skin from the fruits, blanch them first in hot water or use a sharp knife or vegetable peeler.

When cream is served with cooked fruit, it should not be sweetened or whipped; the fruit's syrup will sweeten it enough. My first choice is the top cream from nonhomogenized milk. These fruit dishes improve when they are allowed to macerate for a day or two after baking them.

MELE AL FORNO

Baked Apples

These are not your usual baked apples. They are baked with applejack or other brandy and raisins. Nonno Guiseppe was fond of applejack and produced his own. Following Prohibition, the liquor-licensing laws discouraged him, and from then on he limited production to his own needs. In any case, he left a great dish as part of his culinary legacy.

> 5 apples (Granny Smith)
> ¼ cup golden raisins
> 4 ounces applejack or other brandy
> ⅓ cup sugar
> 1 cinnamon stick
> ¼ cup heavy cream, preferably from the top of nonhomogenized milk (optional)

Preheat the oven to 375° F.

Wash and core the apples. Soak the raisins in the applejack.

Heat 1½ cups water, the sugar, and the cinnamon stick in a baking dish in the oven until the sugar is dissolved. Add the apples to the baking dish and pour the raisins and applejack around them.

Bake the apples until they are tender, for 30 to 50 minutes, depending on the size of the apples. If the apples are cooked before a light syrup develops, remove the apples from the liquid and, if the baking dish is flame-proof, put it over medium heat to reduce the cooking liquid to a syrup. Alternatively, reduce the cooking liquid in a small saucepan.

Serve the apples with 2 or 3 tablespoons of syrup and some cream on the side.

PERE CUCINATE AL VIN ROSSO

PEARS COOKED IN RED WINE

*T*he pears may be poached on top of the stove, but I prefer the oven. They can be prepared in advance and kept in the refrigerator, but should be returned to room temperature or rewarmed before serving.

5 pears
⅓ cup sugar
1 cinnamon stick
¾ cup red wine (not too dry)
¼ cup sweet vermouth or Punt e Mes
¼ cup heavy cream, preferably from the top of nonhomogenized milk (optional)

Preheat the oven to 375° F.

Wash and core the pears. Heat 1 cup of water, the sugar, and cinnamon stick in a flame-proof baking dish over medium heat until the sugar is dissolved and add the red wine, vermouth, and pears. Put the baking dish in the oven and bake the pears until they are tender, for about 45 minutes, turning occasionally. The liquid should reduce to a light syrup.

Serve the pears with 1 or 2 tablespoons of syrup and some cream on the side.

PESCHE CUCINATE

Cooked Peaches

*T*he peaches may be prepared in the same fashion as the pears on page 157. I prefer this preparation with white wine and Amaretto di Saronno or Frangelico, and a sprinkling of nuts at the last moment. If you use Amaretto, sprinkle with sliced almonds. If you use Frangelico, use sliced hazelnuts.

⅓ cup sugar

½ vanilla bean

5 peaches, ripe but firm

½ cup white wine (not dry)

¼ cup Amaretto di Saronno or Frangelico

½ cup sliced almonds or hazelnuts, lightly toasted

¼ cup heavy cream, preferably from the top of nonhomogenized milk (optional)

Preheat the oven to 375° F.

Heat 1 cup water, the sugar, and vanilla bean in a baking dish in the oven until the sugar is dissolved. Cut the peaches in half, remove the pits, and arrange them, cut sides down, in the baking dish. Add the wine and liqueur to the baking dish and return it to the oven. Turn the peaches after 15 minutes. When the peaches are tender, after about 15 more minutes, sprinkle them with the nuts and bake for 2 more minutes. If the peaches are cooked before a light syrup develops, remove them from the liquid and, if the baking dish is flameproof, put it over medium heat to reduce the cooking liquid to a light syrup. Alternatively, reduce the cooking liquid in a small saucepan. Serve the peaches with their syrup and nuts and some cream on the side.

BUDINO DI CASTAGNE

▶▲▼▲▼▲▼▲▼▲◀

Chestnut Pudding
SERVES 4

*F*or this extraordinary dessert, fresh chestnuts are always best, but canned whole chestnuts may be used.

¾ cup sugar

1 cup cooked whole chestnuts (see note below)

3 tablespoons chestnut flour

2 eggs

2 cups milk

¼ teaspoon vanilla extract

¼ teaspoon rum extract

Melt ½ cup of sugar in a saucepan over low heat. Add the chestnuts, stir gently to coat them with the sugar syrup, and remove the pan from the heat. Let the mixture cool. Remove all but 6 chestnuts from the syrup and cut the rest into 3 or 4 pieces each.

As the chestnuts cool, in a bowl mix together the flour, eggs, and ¼ cup milk. Heat the remaining sugar and milk in another pan over medium heat. When the sugar is melted, raise the heat and bring the mixture to a boil, stirring. Slowly stir in the flour mixture, stirring until the mixture is thick enough to coat the back of a spoon. Gently mix in the chestnut pieces. Remove the pan from the heat, add the extracts, and let the pudding cool.

Pour the pudding into a serving dish, decorate with the whole chestnuts, and drizzle with the syrup.

Note: To prepare fresh chestnuts, first slit the shells on the flat side with a sharp knife. Boil or steam the chestnuts for 7 minutes and refresh them under cool water. When cool enough to handle, peel away the shells.

CROSTATE DI FRUTTA
FRUIT TARTS

To make a superior fruit tart, you must make a superb shell. Most European cooks make a version of *Pasta Frolla*, but the formula varies from country to country, province to province, city to city, even house to house. Everyone seems to agree that you need flour, liquid, egg, fat, and salt. The differences are in the flour, liquid, and fat. Nonno Conti insisted on pastry flour, water and half lard (for flakiness) and half butter (for taste). In Val Taro, for a family with only one cow, butter may have been too scarce to use in pastry dough, and to most, lard was unacceptable. A tasty, flaky crust was, and often still is, made with oil. And to conserve wheat flour some chestnut flour may occasionally have been used. Today, we mostly use the recipe here. The variation with chestnut flour is particularly appropriate for an apple tart.

PASTA FROLLA

2½ cups cake flour

2 tablespoons sugar

I teaspoon salt

¼ cup vegetable shortening

4 tablespoons butter cut into pieces

2 extra-large egg yolks or I extra-large whole egg, lightly beaten

3 tablespoons water or liqueur such as Amaretto di Saronno

Put the dry ingredients in a mixing bowl. With your fingertips work the shortening and butter into the dry ingredients until pieces the size of cherries are formed. Add the egg yolks and water and mix the dough into a smooth ball. It may be necessary to knead the dough briefly, but take care not to overwork it. Wrap the dough in plastic wrap or wax paper and put the dough in a cool area or the refrigerator to rest for at least 20 minutes and up to I or 2 days.

Variation: Substitute ½ cup chestnut flour for ½ cup of the cake flour.

Crostata di Mele con Pasta di Castagne

Apple Tart with a Chestnut Shell

*U*pon my father's return from a holiday in Parma, he went on a kick that lasted a lifetime—baking apple tarts the way it is done in the old country. *Grazie*, Mr. C., for this is a wonderful way. Professional bakers often decorate the top with a lattice made from the excess dough; but this style, typical of the country women, is easier and just as artistic.

2 ½ pounds apples such as Granny Smith

⅓ cup sugar

¼ teaspoon ground cinnamon

¼ teaspoon freshly grated nutmeg

2 tablespoons cornstarch or potato flour

1 recipe *Pasta Frolla* made with chestnut flour (page 160)

¼ cup apricot glaze (see note below), warmed

Preheat the oven to 400° F. and butter and flour a 9-inch springform pan.

Peel, core, and slice the apples and put them in a large mixing bowl. Add the sugar, cinnamon, nutmeg, and cornstarch and combine well.

Roll out the dough into a circle about 13 inches in diameter and transfer it to the pan, taking care that it is snug to the edge but not stretching the dough. Fill the shell with the apples, reserving about 15 slices. Fold any excess dough over the fruit and decorate the top with the reserved apple slices arranged in a circle. Bake the tart in the oven for 1 hour, or until the crust is golden brown.

Let the tart cool slightly. With a small brush paint the fruit with the glaze, and remove the tart from the pan.

Note: To make the apricot glaze, purée 1 cup of apricot preserves. Put the purée in a small heavy saucepan with ¼ cup water and simmer over low heat, stirring to dissolve the fruit sugars. Strain the glaze through a fine strainer into a bowl if necessary.

CROSTATA DI PESCHE E FRAGOLE

◀▚▚▚▚▚▚▚▚▶

PEACH AND
STRAWBERRY TART

*I*n the Apennines, this is made with the wild strawberries that grow in the mountains. An additional ½ pound of peaches may be substituted for the strawberries. The variation below is my favorite *crostata*.

> 2 pounds peaches
> 1 pint strawberries
> 2 to 3 tablespoons sugar, depending on the sweetness of the fruit
> 2 tablespoons cornstarch or potato flour
> 1 recipe *Pasta Frolla* (page 160)
> ¼ cup apricot glaze (Note, page 161), warmed

Preheat the oven to 400° F. and butter and flour a 9-inch springform pan.

Wash and slice the peaches and put them in a bowl. Clean and hull the strawberries; reserve 3 or 4. Slice the strawberries in half and add them to the sliced peaches. Add the sugar and cornstarch and combine well.

Roll out the dough into a circle about 13 inches in diameter and transfer it to the pan, taking care that it is snug to the edge but not stretching the dough. Fill the shell with the peach and strawberry mixture, reserving 12 slices of peaches. Fold any excess dough over the fruit or roll it down to form an edge. Decorate the top with the reserved peach slices arranged in a circle. Bake the tart in the oven for 1 hour, or until the crust is golden brown.

Let the tart cool slightly. With a small brush paint the fruit with the glaze, and remove the tart from the pan. Dip the reserved strawberries into some remaining glaze and make a design in the middle.

VARIATION: CROSTATA DI FRUTTA MISTA

MIXED FRUIT TART

I generally make this with peaches, plums, and strawberries, but you can increase the complexity with additional fruits. Cherries, paticularly the sour variety, give an interesting dimension. Use a total of 2½ pounds of mixed fruits and berries, sliced.

Pan di Spagna con Crema Pasticciera

❧❧❧❧❧❧❧❧

Spanish Bread with Pastry Cream

Spongecake and pastry cream form the bases for different desserts. In the hamlets of Val Taro they are combined to make a simple sweet that takes advantage of their natural tastes and textures.

FOR THE CAKE:

  2 cups all-purpose flour
  Zest of 1 lemon
  ¼ teaspoon salt
  1⅛ cups sugar
  5 eggs
  2 teaspoons vanilla extract

FOR THE PASTRY CREAM:

  ¼ cup cake flour
  1 tablespoon cornstarch
  ½ teaspoon salt
  4 extra-large eggs
  3 cups milk
  1 cup sugar
  1 tablespoon vanilla extract
  8 tablespoons butter (optional)

Preheat the oven to 350° F. and butter and flour two 9-inch baking pans.

To make the cake: Sift the flour into a bowl, add the lemon zest, and mix in the salt. Put the sugar, eggs, and vanilla in a mixing bowl and with an electric mixer beat together until they increase to about 4 times their volume and form soft peaks. Fold the flour mixture into the egg mixture by sprinkling it lightly over as you fold. Pour the batter into the pans and bake the cake layers in the oven for 30 minutes, or until a toothpick inserted into the center of the cake layers comes out clean.

To make the pastry cream: Sift the cake flour, cornstarch, and salt into a bowl. Whisk in the eggs and ½ cup of the milk, mixing well. Mix the remaining milk and the sugar in a heavy saucepan over medium-high heat. Bring the milk to the scalding point and lower the heat to keep the milk warm.

(continued)

Whisk the flour and egg mixture again and slowly mix it into the hot milk. Cook the mixture, stirring until the whisk leaves lines in the pastry cream. Remove the pan from the heat and stir in the vanilla extract and butter. Pour the pastry cream into a heatproof glass dish or container and cover it with buttered wax paper. When it is cooled to room temperature, store the pastry cream, covered with wax paper, in the refrigerator.

PASTICCINI

MINIATURE PASTRIES

*P*arma's pastries are on a par with its famous cheese. Among the favorites are the miniature pastries found in pastry shops. Most home kitchens are without tiny tart pans for mini-tarts, but upside-down mini-muffin tins are perfect for producing 24 tarts.

FOR THE *PASTA FROLLA*:

> 3½ cups cake flour
> 5 tablespoons vegetable shortening
> 5 tablespoons butter
> 5 tablespoons sugar
> 1 teaspoon salt
> 4 egg yolks or 2 extra-large whole eggs
> 2 tablespoons cold water
> 2 tablespoons dry white wine

To make the pastry dough: Using the ingredients given above, follow the instructions for preparing *Pasta Frolla* (page 160).

Preheat the oven to 425° F.

Roll out the dough ⅛ inch thick. Use a cookie cutter to cut out 24 disks 2¾ inches in diameter. Invert the muffin tin and fit the disks of dough over the bottoms of the muffin forms. Alternatively, the dough can be fitted into tiny individual tart pans. Bake the tart shells until they are golden brown, about 15 minutes.

Carefully remove the tart shells from the muffin tin and cool them on a wire rack.

PASTICCINI DI FRAGOLE

Miniature Strawberry Tarts

MAKES 8 MINIATURE PASTRIES

FOR THE TARTS:

⅓ cup strawberry preserves
⅔ cup pastry cream (page 163)
8 miniature tart shells (page 164)

FOR THE DIPPING CHOCOLATE:

½ cup sugar
½ teaspoon light corn syrup
½ teaspoon butter
3 to 4 tablespoons milk
1 ounce unsweetened chocolate

FOR DECORATING TARTS:

8 large whole strawberries
½ cup whipped cream (optional)

To make the tarts: Stir the preserves into the pastry cream until the mixture has a marbleized appearance and divide it among the tart shells.

To make the dipping chocolate: Put the sugar, corn syrup, butter, and 3 tablespoons milk into a heavy saucepan, bring to a simmer, and simmer the mixture, stirring, for 5 to 6 minutes. Remove the pan from the heat when the mixture is thick enough to coat the back of a spoon and stir in the chocolate. The chocolate is ready for dipping when it has a smooth, velvety, shiny texture and there are no more specks of chocolate. To maintain the proper consistency, set the pan over another pan of hot but still water. If the chocolate becomes too thick to work with, return to low heat and whisk in the remaining tablespoon of milk.

To decorate the tarts: Dip the strawberries into the chocolate and arrange 1 strawberry in the center of each tart. Using a pastry bag fitted with a star tip, make a border of whipped cream around the edge of each tart.

Variations: The strawberries can be coated with warmed apricot glaze (Note, page 161) rather than chocolate; store-bought dipping chocolate may also be used.

Pasticcini di Lamponi

❮❮❮❮❮❮❮❮❮❮❮

Miniature
Raspberry Tarts

MAKES 8 MINIATURE
PASTRIES

½ teaspoon almond extract
¼ cup pastry cream (page 163)
8 miniature tart shells (page 164)
4 heaping tablespoons raspberry preserves
4 tablespoons sliced almonds
3 tablespoons honey
3 tablespoons dipping chocolate (page 165), warmed

Mix the almond extract into the pastry cream and divide the mixture among the tart shells. Fill each shell to the top with the preserves and top with the almonds. Drizzle the honey over the almonds with a swirling movement and drizzle the dipping chocolate in the same way.

Pasticcini di Ciliegie

❮❮❮❮❮❮❮❮❮❮❮

Miniature
Cherry Tarts

MAKES 8 MINIATURE
PASTRIES

⅔ cups pastry cream (page 163)
8 miniature tart shells (page 164)
1⅓ cup pitted fresh sweet cherries
Apricot glaze (Note, page 161), warmed

Chop ⅔ cup of the cherries. Combine the pastry cream and chopped cherries in a bowl and divide the mixture among the tart shells. Top the tarts with the remaining cherries and using a small brush paint the fruit with the glaze.

Variations: Brandied cherries, sautéed for 30 seconds, or drained canned cherries may be substituted for fresh ones.

FRAGOLE MILLEFOGLIE

Strawberry Napoleon

*T*he pastry for this and other napoleons—*millefoglie*, meaning a thousand leaves, or layers—takes hours to make, but the hands-on effort is minimal. Plan ahead and organize the chores involved, and you will find the process easy, even enjoyable; and the results are outstanding.

The many layers are created by rolling and folding the dough several times. In the process, fat is trapped in the flour, which accounts for the pastry's ultimate crispness and flakiness.

> **2 cups flour**
> **½ teaspoon salt**
> **5 tablespoons vegetable shortening**
> **5 tablespoons butter**
> **⅓ cup ice water**
> **I egg**
> **1½ cups pastry cream (page 163)**
> **I pint strawberries, cleaned and hulled**
> **Apricot glaze (Note, page 161), warmed**

Mix together the flour and salt in a mixing bowl. With your fingertips work the shortening and butter into the flour until pieces the size of walnuts are formed. Add enough of the water to work the dough into a ball, but take care not to overwork it. If the dough seems oily or sticky, dust it all over with flour. Wrap the dough in wax paper and refrigerate for at least 45 minutes and up to overnight.

Generously flour a work surface. Roll out the dough to form a rectangle about 10- by 14 inches and fold into thirds as you would a business letter. If the dough sticks to the work surface, pick up each end, I at a time, and reflour the work surface. Wrap the folded dough in wax paper and refrigerate for at least 45 minutes. Roll out and fold the dough at least 3 more times, refrigerating in between and again before baking.

Preheat the oven to 425° F.

Roll out the dough to form a 14- by 8-inch rectangle about ⅛ inch thick and prick all over with a fork. To make a raised edge on the napoleon, cut four ½-inch-wide slices lengthwise and four ½-inch-wide slices crosswise. Transfer the rectangle to a baking sheet.

Make an egg wash by beating the egg with 2 teaspoons of water. To build the pastry edges, using a small brush paint the pastry strips with some of the egg wash and place 2 strips on each edge of the pastry rectangle. Paint the entire pastry with the remaining egg wash. Bake the pastry in the oven until golden brown, about 30 to 45 minutes, watching closely so that it does not overcook or burn.

Remove the pastry from the oven and allow to cool. Put a layer of pastry cream over the inside of the napoleon and arrange the strawberries on the pastry cream, points up. Using another small brush paint the strawberries with the glaze.

The bars and *gelaterie* of Parma offer such a variety of tastes that I have been compelled to make my own. *Gelato di crema* is made with egg-enriched milk; the base is really a custard. Natural flavors, fortified or not, are added. The results of the recipes that follow are almost identical to the Parmesan originals. The minor differences probably can be attributed to variations in the milk.

Sorbetto is another matter. Made without milk and only a little egg white, it is full of the fresh taste of fruit, enhanced perhaps with a small amount of wine or liqueur.

I recommend an ice-cream machine to make *gelato* or *sorbetto*. Otherwise, the foundations must be taken in and out of the freezer a few times and whisked before it freezes, but you still can get good results.

GELATO ALLA VANIGLIA

Vanilla Gelato

YIELDS 3 CUPS

2¼ cups milk
½ vanilla bean, finely minced or pulverized, with seeds
4 egg yolks
½ cup sugar
I teaspoon vanilla extract

Mix together ¼ cup of the milk and the vanilla bean in a saucepan and scald the milk. Beat the egg yolks and sugar together in the top of a double boiler or in a metal bowl that will fit over a pan. Scald the remaining milk in another pan and slowly mix it into the egg mixture. In the double boiler or bowl set over a hot pan of slowly simmering water that does not touch the underside, cook the mixture, stirring, until it is thick enough to coat the back of a spoon. Add the vanilla bean and milk mixture to the custard. Remove the double boiler or pan from the heat, let the mixture cool, and chill it thoroughly in the refrigerator. Add the vanilla extract to the mixture and freeze in an ice-cream machine according to the manufacturer's instructions. Transfer the *gelato* to a container and store in the freezer for several hours or overnight.

GELATO DI CREMA CARAMELLA

Caramel Gelato

YIELDS 3 CUPS

2½ tablespoons butter

¾ cup sugar

4 egg yolks

2 cups milk

¼ cup sweet Marsala

Melt 1½ tablespoons of the butter in a saucepan and add ½ cup of the sugar. Simmer the mixture, stirring. When the sugar begins to brown, add ½ cup of water and cook until the sugar is dissolved. When the caramel becomes a deep mahogany color, remove the pan from the heat.

Put the egg yolks in the top of a double boiler or in a metal bowl that wiil fit over a saucepan and whisk lightly. Scald the milk in a pan and slowly mix it into the egg yolks. Mix the caramel into the egg mixture. In the double boiler or bowl set over a pan of slowly simmering water that does not touch the underside, cook the mixture, stirring, until it is thick enough to coat the back of a spoon. Remove the double boiler or pan from the heat, let the mixture cool, and chill it thoroughly in the refrigerator.

Melt the remaining butter in a sauté pan, add the remaining sugar, and stir until the sugar begins to brown. Add the Marsala and stir to dissolve the sugar. Cool the mixture in the refrigerator and add it to the egg mixture. Put the mixture in an ice-cream machine and freeze according to the manufacturer's instructions. Transfer the *gelato* to a container and store in the freezer for several hours or overnight.

GELATO DI RUM E SULTANINE

Rum Raisin Gelato

YIELDS 3 CUPS

¼ cup sultana raisins

¼ cup light rum

4 egg yolks

½ cup sugar

¼ teaspoon salt

2 cups milk

1 teaspoon rum extract

Soak the raisins in the rum.

Mix together the egg yolks, sugar, and salt in the top of a double boiler or in a metal bowl that will fit over a saucepan. Scald the milk in another pan and slowly pour it into the egg mixture, stirring rapidly. In the double boiler or bowl set over a pan of slowly simmering water that does not touch the underside, cook the mixture, stirring, until it is thick enough to coat the back of a spoon. Remove the double boiler or pan from the heat, let the mixture cool, and chill it thoroughly in the refrigerator.

Put the rum and raisins in a pan over low heat, simmer the mixture for no more than 10 seconds, and cool it in the refrigerator.

Stir the rum mixture and rum extract into the egg mixture and freeze in an ice-cream machine according to the manufacturer's instructions. Transfer the *gelato* to a container and store in the freezer for several hours or overnight.

SORBETTO DI FRAGOLE

STRAWBERRY SORBET

YIELDS 4 CUPS

1 quart strawberries

¼ cup sugar

1 cup white wine (not dry)

Strained juice of ½ lemon

¼ egg white

Clean, hull, and cut the strawberries into rough halves or quarters, depending on their size. Put the strawberries, sugar, wine, lemon juice, and ¼ cup water in a saucepan and bring the mixture to a boil. Remove the pan from the heat and let the mixture cool. Purée the mixture in a food processor.

Beat the egg white until it forms soft peaks and fold it into the strawberry mixture. Put the mixture in an ice-cream machine and freeze according to the manufacturer's directions. Transfer the *sorbetto* to a container and store in the freezer for several hours or overnight.

SORBETTO DI MELE

Apple Sorbet

YIELDS 4 CUPS

4 apples (Granny Smith)
¼ cup sugar
¼ cup brandy such as applejack
1 tablespoon Amaretto di Saronno
1 teaspoon almond extract
¼ egg white

Peel, core, and slice the apples.

Put the apples, sugar, and ¼ cup water in a saucepan over medium heat. Slowly boil the mixture, covered, until the apples are soft, adding more water if necessary. Add the brandy and simmer the mixture 1 minute (take care as the mixture may ignite). Add the Amaretto.

Remove the pan from the heat, let the mixture cool to room temperature, and purée it in a food processor. Transfer the purée to a bowl and add the almond extract. Beat the egg white until it forms stiff peaks and fold it into the apple mixture. Put the mixture in an ice-cream machine and freeze according to the manufacturer's instructions. Transfer the *sorbetto* to a container and store in the freezer for several hours or overnight.

TORTA DI GELATO

ICE-CREAM CAKE
16 TO 18 SERVINGS

This is a glamorous and festive sweet for special occasions. This dish was quite a popular dessert at Camillo Restaurant, and at one time I made eight or nine cakes a week. I normally line the pan with the *gelato* and *sorbetto* and cake one day and freeze it overnight, then finish with the *zabaione* the next.

> I recipe *Pan di Spagna* (page 163; omit pastry cream)
> I recipe *Gelato di Vaniglia* (page 169)
> I recipe *Sorbetto di Fragole* (page 162)
> I recipe cold *Zabaione Parmigiano*

FOR THE *ZABAIONE PARMIGIANO*:

> I cup heavy cream
> 4½ tablespoons sugar
> I teaspoon vanilla extract
> 8 egg yolks
> ½ cup sweet Marsala
> I ounce light rum
> ⅓ cup mixed candied fruit

Cut the cake into ¼-inch-thick slices and reserve them.

Line the inside of a 3-quart bundt pan with the *gelato* and the *sorbetto*, working from the center of the pan up to the rim and alternating flavors to create a pinwheel design. Put the pan in the freezer to set the *gelato* and *sorbetto*. When they are set, make a layer with the reserved cake slices, cutting and fitting them as necessary to cover the frozen layer entirely. If the *gelato* and *sorbetto* begin to soften so that they are no longer holding their shape, return the pan to the freezer. Cover the pan with plastic wrap or aluminum foil and place it in the freezer for several hours or overnight.

To make the *zabaione*: Whip the heavy cream in a cold bowl until it triples in volume and forms soft peaks. Beat in I tablespoon of the sugar and the vanilla and put the mixture in the refrigerator.

Put the egg yolks, the remaining sugar, Marsala, and rum in a double boiler or in a metal bowl that will fit over a pan of simmering water that does not touch the underside. Whip the yolk mixture for 30 seconds to incorporate some air. Continue whipping until the mixture increases to about 4 times its volume and clings to the side of the top of the double boiler or bowl. Do not let the mixture come close to a boil or the eggs will curdle. Remove the double boiler or pan from the heat, and set it in a larger pan of ice, and mix the *zabaione* until it is cold. When the *zabaione* is cold, fold in the whipped cream and candied fruits. Pour the *zabaione* into the cavity of the frozen cake. If the *zabaione* does not completely fill the cavity, put the pan in the freezer to set the *zabaione* and fill the remaining space with vanilla *gelato*. Store the cake in the freezer, covered with plastic wrap, overnight or up to 2 weeks.

To serve the cake: Unmold the cake by quickly submerging the pan up to the rim in hot water. Cover the pan with a serving plate, invert it, and gently lift the pan off the cake. If necessary, the cake can be returned to the freezer for a few hours before serving.

MENUS

Simple Meals

Many of the dishes in this book have been daily fare for Parmigiani going back many generations. It may come as a surprise to learn that the time and means for preparing meals were probably as restricted one hundred years ago as they are today. But that was indeed the case, and meals that could be cooked in one pot, letting the fire do the work, or executed by quick methods such as sautéing and grilling were necessities. Today, of course, we also have advanced kitchen equipment, which, along with a bit of strategic planning, can help put good meals on the table even on busy weekdays.

The Sidolis are a typical contemporary family. My mother, Marie, had a demanding career in New York City's fashion industry, yet managed to maintain her culinary standards even during the week of a "showing." The younger generation is represented by my son Richard and his wife, Diane, who are carrying on the Parmesan traditions.

The menus that follow are examples of meals we cook for ourselves. I've included some tips on organizing the chores involved so that good, simple everyday meals can be executed efficiently. Nonna Vecchia and Zia Maria gave us the basics, along with the recipes, and I am happy to be able to pass them along.

In this robust meal, the preparation of the vegetables is the most time-consuming element, so start by cleaning and cooking them. Then sauté the beef and prepare the risotto.

Risotto al Vin Rosso
Risotto with Red Wine (page 32)
Bistecca Fritta al Vin Rosso
Beef Steak Sautéed in Red Wine (page 87)
Barbabietole e Cime di Barbabietole
Beets and Beet Greens (page 125)

This meal requires but 15 minutes of work and is on the table within an hour.

Pezzi di Pollo con Patate e Funghi al Forno
Chicken Baked with Potatoes and Mushrooms (page 107)

The beef and pears can be cooked a day in advance, and the *gnocchi* prepared up to the point of boiling, then frozen overnight. The beef can also be cooked in a pressure cooker. You can plan ahead for another meal by making extra beef to use as filling for ravioli or "veal birds."

Brasato di Manzo della Val Taro
Potted Beef from the Val Taro (page 84)
Pere Cucinate al Vin Rosso
Pears Cooked in Red Wine (page 157)

Start cooking the zucchini, then the risotto. Finally, sauté the trout. This meal is easily on the table in 45 minutes.

Risotto al Vin Bianco e Piselli
Risotto with White Wine and Peas (page 38)
Trota all'Aceto Rosso
Trout and Red-Wine Vinegar (page 116)
Zucchini e Funghi con Aceto
Zucchini and Mushrooms with Vinegar (page 122)

This can be made with extra pot roast and you can have yet another meal at the ready if you make additional ravioli and store them in your freezer.

Ravioli di Manzo Brasato e Spinaci con Salsa di Funghi e Sugo
Pot Roast and Spinach Ravioli (page 50) with Mushroom Sauce with a Hint of Meat Essence (page 60)
Insalata di Cavolo di Savoia e Fagioli
Salad of Savoy cabbage and beans (page 140)

This one-pot meal is ready in an hour. Fruit and cheese make a perfect ending.

Minestra di Riso e Cavolo
Rice and Cabbage *Minestra* (page 67)

OVERLEAF: *A Simple Meal: Clockwise from right, Dandelion Salad with Egg, Robust Veal Casserole with Polenta, Baked Apples*

Start the sauce, prepare the salad, then cook the polenta according to the faster technique in the recipe. Grilled luganega or a similar sausage can be added to the meal, which can be ready in about 30 minutes.

Polenta con Ragù al Forno
Baked Polenta with Ragù (page 30)
Insalata di Finocchio e Sedano
Fennel and Celery Salad (page 139)

This hearty meatless meal can be on the table in about an hour or just a bit longer. Start the minestra, then make the salad.

Minestra Con Piselli e Spinaci
Pea and Spinach *Minestra* (page 72)
Insalata di Barbabietole e Patate
Beet and Potato Salad (page 142)

Again, a low-fat vegetarian meal that takes only about an hour to prepare. If you have not made the apples in advance, put them into the oven with the eggplant. It will all cook together.

Melanzane Ripiene al Forno
Baked Stuffed Eggplant (page 127)
Insalata di Cicoria di Campo con Uova
Dandelion and Egg Salad (page 143)
Mele al Forno
Baked Apples (page 156)

Once the stuffed peppers have been put into the oven, prepare the salad.

Peperoni Ripieni di Riso al Forno
Baked Rice-Stuffed Peppers (page 130)
Insalata di Indivia Riccia
Chicory Salad (page 144)

After the broth is added to the cacciatora, make the salad, then the polenta. A farm-raised rabbit or chicken will take about 45 minutes (or less) to cook, a wild rabbit may take longer.

Coniglio alla Cacciatora con Polenta o Pollo alla Cacciatora
Rabbit "Hunter's Style" with Polenta (page 105) or Chicken "Hunter's Style" (page 106)
Insalata di Capricciosa
Mixed Raw Vegetables (page 145)

Clean the spinach and assemble the veal; begin to sauté the veal, then finish the spinach. I include the sorbet when I have it in my freezer.

Involtini di Vitello
Stuffed Veal Envelopes (page 95)
Spinaci alla Parmigiana
Creamed Spinach Parmesan Style (page 123)
Sorbetto di Fragole
Strawberry Sorbet (page 172)

arinate the vegetables and the meat for 10 minutes, then put everything except the tomato on the grill. Move the vegetables and steak to 1 side of the grill as they cook; put the tomatoes on when everything else is about half-done.

Fette di Vitello alla Griglia
Grilled Veal Steaks (page 96)
Patate, Zucchini, Asparagi, e Pomodori alla
   Griglia
Grilled Potato, Zucchini, Asparagus, and Tomato

he cooking time here is about 2 hours, but the hands-on work is only 15 to 20 minutes, so this is a good meal to plan in advance. Only the salad and the final cooking needs to be done right before serving.

Cotechino con Polenta
Cotechino with Polenta (page 99)
Insalata Capricciosa
Mixed Raw Vegetables (page 145)
Ida's Focaccia di Fecola di patate
Ida's Potato Flour Cake (page 149)

his takes about 45 minutes. Begin with the zucchini, then the risotto. Finally, sauté the trout.

Risotto al Vin Bianco e Piselli
Risotto with White Wine and Peas (page 38)
Trota All'Aceto Rosso
Trout and Red Wine Vinegar (page 116)
Zucchine e Funghi con Aceto
Zucchini and Mushrooms with Vinegar (page
   122)

egin by cooking the gnocchi, then make the mushrooms, and, finally, the salad. This meal takes me about 45 minutes.

Gnocchi di Patate con Funghi
Gnocchi with Mushroom Sauce (page 57)
Insalata di Lattuga Romana e Parmigiano
Romaine Lettuce and Parmigiano (page 146)

ut 2 pots of water on to boil for the pasta and the turnips, then finish the antipasto. The fish is baked last; in fact, it can go into the oven when the pasta is served.

Antipasto di Rape e Pomodori
White Turnip and Tomato Antipasto (page 16)
Tagliatelle Verdi con Parmigiano
Spinach Pasta with Cheese (page 41)
Pesce Gatto al Forno
Baked Catfish (page 117)

his elegant meal can be on the table in 30 to 40 minutes. The rollatini are quick and easy to prepare with excess filling from stuffed pasta and nicely balanced by the fennel and peas flavors.

Uccelli di Vitello
Veal "Birds" (page 97)
Finocchio e Piselli in Padella
Sautéed Fennel and Peas (page 138)

CLASSIC MENUS

The classic dishes of Parma were the the ones aristocrats in bygone days enjoyed often. For my Parmesan ancestors, these were dishes for special occasions; they were passed on to my family for the most part by Nonno Guiseppe. These classics were first served in the United States by my relatives in the mid-1890s, and they are as elegant today as they were then.

This was the favorite of my father, Camillo. If all the dinners he served were put on exhibit, this is the one he would gravitate to.

> Carciofi Ripieni
> Stuffed Artichokes (page 20)
> Risotto con Ragù della Val Taro
> Risotto with Meat Sauce (page 34)
> Petto di Vitello Ripieno di Camillo
> Camillo's Stuffed Breast of Veal (page 90)
> Finocchio Brasato
> Braised Fennel (page 138)
> Pomodori Ripieni al Forno
> Baked Stuffed Tomatoes (page 131)
> Insalata di Indivia Riccia
> Chicory Salad (page 144)
> Crostata di Mele con Pasta di Castagne
> Apple Tart with a Chestnut Shell (page 161)

The pastry dough for the apple tart may be prepared ahead, as can the filling for the breast of veal. The artichokes can be readied for stuffing, or even stuffed ahead of time as well. Of course, the ragù may be prepared up to several days in advance.

Here is a classic menu that blends the dishes from the city of Parma and the nearby mountain region of Val Taro; it is a relatively easy menu to put together and excellent for entertaining family and friends.

> Torta di Spinaci, Torta di Zucca
> Spinach *Torta* (page 10), Squash *Torta* (page 14)
> Lasagne in Bianca
> White Lasagne (page 58)
> Vitello Arrosto con Verdure Miste
> Roast Veal with Roast Mixed Vegetables (page 92)
> Funghi Ripieni al Forno
> Stuffed Mushrooms (page 126)
> Crostata di Pesche e Fragole
> Peach and Strawberry Tart (page 162)

The dough and fillings for the *torte* may be made in advance; just roll out the dough, fill, and bake them the day they are to be served. The lasagne may be assembled a day in advance, then baked when needed. If the dessert isn't prepared the day before it should be the first thing in the oven. Put the veal and vegetables in the oven, then prepare and bake the mushrooms. If you wish to include a salad, prepare it last.

Traditionally this is an ideal Easter Sunday dinner, though some families prefer *capretto*—the word for kid, or baby goat.

Torta di Patate, Asparagi Conditi con Olio, Limone, e Aceto Rosso, Antipasti di Rapa e Pomodori, Funghi Marinati

Potato *Torta* (page 13), Asparagus Vinaigrette (page 21), White Turnip and Tomato Antipasto (page 16), Marinated Mushrooms (page 5)

Risotto Robusto

Robust Risotto (page 37)

Cosciotto di Agnello Arrostito con Erbe Aromatiche

Herbed Roast Leg of Lamb (page 101)

Carote

Carrots (page 137)

Flan di Spinaci alla Parmigiana

Spinach Soufflé Parmesan Style (page 124)

Crostata di Ricotta

Cheesecake (page 150)

Marinate the mushrooms for 1 or 2 days. Make the *torta* dough and the filling in advance, and simply roll, fill, and bake it the day of the meal. A whole leg of lamb takes more than 3½ hours to roast and set, so on the day of your dinner, first put the lamb in the oven. The cake may be baked very early—before the lamb goes intot he oven— or the day before. Cook the asparagus and the turnips, and prepare the sauce (or make the sauce a day or so in advance). Prepare the soufflé and bake it as soon as the lamb comes out of the oven. The lamb should be kept in a warm, draft-free spot until it is served. Cook the carrots and begin the preparation of the risotto.

With some seasonal adjustments to replace the asparagus and peaches needed for the dessert, this becomes a traditional Christmas menu.

Pâté di Parma, Torta di Riso, e Torta di Cavolo di Savoia

Parma's Liver Pâté (page 6), Rice *Torta* (page 12), and Savoy Cabbage *Torta* (page 15)

Anulin in Brodo

Anulin in Broth (page 77)

Cappone Arrostito Ripieno di Spinaci

Roasted Capon with Spinach Stuffing (page 115)

Patate Arrostite con Erbe Aromatiche

Roasted Potatoes with Aromatic Herbs (page 135)

Asparagi alla Parmigiana

Asparagus Parmesan Style (page 132)

Crostata di Pesche

Peach Tart (page 162)

The *anulin* can be made up to a month in advance and stored in the freezer. Otherwise, make the filling a day or so ahead and the dough on the day of your dinner. The broth and the pâté can both be made several days ahead.

The peach tart can be assembled the day before your dinner then put into the oven first, followed by the rice and cabbage *torte*, then the capon and roasted potatoes. Prepare the vegetables and finish all dishes according to the recipes.

Traditionally, this was a menu for fall and winter, often enjoyed once the hogs were dressed for curing. Today, it is delightful twelve months a year with minor seasonal adjustments.

Pâté di Parma
Parma's Liver Pâté (page 6)
Torta di Cavolo di Savoia
Savoy Cabbage *Torta* (page 15)
Antipasti Assortiti
Assorted Appetizers (page 17)
Cannelloni
Cannelloni (page 54)
Arista di Maiale Arrosto
Roast Loin of Pork (page 98)
Patate Arrostite con Erbe Aromatiche
Roast Potatoes with Aromatic Herbs (page 135)
Broccoli alla Parmigiana
Broccoli Parmesan Style (page 133)
Mele al Forno
Baked Apples (page 156)
Ida's Focaccia di Fecola di Patate
Ida's Potato Flour Cake (page 149)

For this menu, the *cannelloni* are prepared in advance, ready to be sauced and baked. The baked apples are best if they are cooked a day or so in advance. Serve them cold, at room temperature, or reheated.

To start cooking the day of the party, first put Ida's cake in the oven. Prepare the filling for the *torta* a day in advance, then assemble it while the cake bakes. Put the *torta* and the roast in the oven after the cake is removed (the flexible and forgiving *torta* can cook at this slightly lower temperature). Start preparing the vegetables and follow the recipes to finish all preparations.

At first glance, this menu might seem more American or "continental" than Italian, but in fact Parmesans were enjoying onion soup and roasted meat long before Europeans found their way to the New World. Today, roast beef is not uncommon on Parma's dining tables—at home or in restaurants—and also is offered in specialty food shops.

Torta di Spinaci
Spinach *Torta* (page 10)
Antipasti Assortiti
Assorted Appetizers (page 17)
Funghi Marinate
Marinated Mushrooms (page 5)
Zuppa di Cipolle al Forno
Baked Onion Soup (page 76)
Arrosto di Manzo
Roast Beef (page 86)
Zucchini alla Parmigiana
Zucchini Parmesan (page 122)
Flan di Zucca
Squash Soufflé (page 141)
Insalata di Lattuga Romana e Parmigiano
Romaine Lettuce and Shaved Parmigiano
    (page 146)
Tiramisù
"Pick-me-up" (page 152)
Pere Cucinate al Vin Rosso
Pears Cooked in Red Wine (page 157)

Both the *tiramisù* and the pears are best prepared a day or so before they are served. The marinated mushrooms and the broth for the onion soup should be made a few days in advance. For this menu, I use loin strip of beef.

Put the *torta* in the oven and start preparing the vegetables. Put the roast in the oven about 2 to 3 hours before dinner is to be served, so that it cooks and sets properly.

INDEX